ORLINE D. FOSTER'S

The Art of Tape Reading

TICKER TECHNIQUE

REVISED & EDITED BY

DR. ROBERT H. PERSONS, JR. (*Associate Professor of Economics* at University of Bridgeport)

WITH ADDITIONAL MATERIAL BY

DON WORDEN (Editor of Worden Tape Reading Studies)

and

HERBERT LIESNER (Tape Analyst for Indicator Digest, Inc.)

TABLE OF CONTENTS

PART IV

TRADING WITH TICKER TECHNIQUE

LIST OF TABLES

LIST OF CHARTS

The

Art

of

Tape

Reading

TICKER
TECHNIQUE

Part One

THE MECHANICS OF THE TAPE

1

INTRODUCTION – WHAT YOU CAN ACCOMPLISH WITH TICKER TECHNIQUE

Timing—when to buy and when to sell—is the essential ingredient in any successful investment program. Painstaking investigations into earnings and the balance sheets can usually pinpoint several stocks that appear sound and "undervalued" in almost any market, but commitments can prove frustrating if the market simply ignores these situations even though they seem dirt cheap. Your stock should have a story to tell, but the market has to be ready to listen.

If you want to know how the market evaluates a stock, watch the tape. Never argue with the tape. *Stocks are worth what they sell for.* Bankers accept this judgment when they lend money on stocks. The Internal Revenue Service will accept the judgment of the tape if you are going to take profits out of the market on a regular basis.

Although the judgment of the tape is final and irrevocable, an important decision is seldom rendered without some preliminary debate. Learning to follow the preliminary skirmishes that ultimately deliver a market verdict is the only sure road to correct timing of investments. Admittedly, some of these preliminary skirmishes may prove inconclusive or become aggravatingly protracted; but there seems no real alternative to asking the market, as patiently as possible, how it plans to evaluate a stock.

3

An approach built solely on "ought to sell at such-and-such a price" is mere guesswork or wishful thinking. True, it can produce stock market profits on occasion, but it can lead to shocking losses, too. Investment programs built close to the hardpan reality of market action have less distance to fall when they go haywire and are usually more surefooted when they march along the indicated trend.

The market speaks with a two-word vocabulary—price and volume. Any attempt to understand market action must start with an appreciation of all of the subtle things price and volume can say about it. The art of translating the patterns of price and volume into meaningful statements about the probable course of future action is "tape-reading."

Tape-reading has often been made to sound mysterious. Some tape-readers themselves are unaware of exactly how they learned their art and are at a loss when asked to express their techniques in a few simple rules. However, by paying very close attention to the way tape-readers act, how they size up a situation, and what they say they are doing, it is possible to spell out—in broad terms, at least—what may be called "ticker technique."

The term "ticker technique" has been chosen to provide a short-hand designation for the stock market trading procedures outlined in this book chiefly because the alternative term, "tape-reading," is sometimes limited to a very specialized method—buying and selling solely on the evidence of price and volume on the tape. In practice, few tape-readers take such a narrow view of their method; they consider many other factors in arriving at a decision to buy or sell. But if the final, deciding factor is the action of price and volume—hourly, daily, or weekly —this is tape-reading as generally practiced and the application of ticker technique as the term is used in this book.

If you watch the reaction of price and volume to a reported earnings rise, a new product, or a stock-split rumor, then you are using ticker technique. On the other hand, if you buy a stock solely on the basis of a projected earnings rise, a new product, or a stock-split rumor, you are not making use of the information that can be provided by ticker technique. It will be the purpose of this book to demonstrate how an understanding of the interplay between news and the ticker can better govern your market moves and improve the chances of their success in a reasonable time span.

Properly used, ticker technique can provide valuable insight into the inner workings of the market, but it is a skill that must be acquired through constant practice. Nothing can take the place of a practical application, by you yourself, of these general techniques and rules to individual stocks. Little can be learned from studying these methods unless you are willing to devote the time necessary to a review of the reported price and volume figures.

After thoroughly mastering some of the basic concepts of ticker technique and acquiring some proficiency in applying these concepts to the mass of trading details that run along the tape every day, there is a very rewarding experience in store for you: you will be in a position to turn a deaf ear to tips, rumors, and many other types of investment advice that have probably only confused you in the past. Or, you can still listen to the tipsters; they are sometimes very compelling. But at least you will be in a position to run an independent test: you can see what the stock ticker has to say.

There are three ways to "read" the tape:

1. Transaction-by-transaction (as it comes over the electronic board or paper tape), with pad and pencil in hand.

2. Reconstruction of the tape. Some transactions take place on declining prices (downticks); others on rising prices (upsticks); some are in standard 100-share units; others in big blocks. These details can be sorted out according to some preconceived notion of what is significant. This can be done from the actual tape or from the data supplied by one of the price record services.

3. Summary data, daily and weekly. High-low-close and volume figures are reported in most of the large metropolitan dailies, as well as *The Wall Street Journal* (daily) and *Barron's* (weekly). These handy summaries of tape action can be used to study trends.

All three of these approaches are widely employed. Which you choose will probably depend largely on the time you have available. With a full-time job, it would obviously be impractical to consider watching the live tape. Even going over complete listings of daily sales would put a considerable strain on the time of the average person. As a result, many investors look for their price and volume readings in the daily or weekly summary tables.

Of course, much detail is lost in the summaries (for a rundown of some of the details available only by following every single transaction, see Chapters 9 and 10 in Part III). But there are some tape-readers who feel that more perspective can be maintained by not following every trade. They make sure of their most important decisions away from the actual tape, looking at the individual trades only in certain circumstances.

All three approaches will be discussed. Often an insight from one approach can be successfully adapted to another. Whatever approach you decide to adopt, it should be fitted to your own temperament and time available. It is better to do less but do it thoroughly than to fall hopelessly behind by attempting too much.

All three approaches deal in four classes of facts:
1. Price—levels, supports, breakouts.
2. Volume—evidence of accumulation or distribution.
3. Breadth—degree of participation in the current move.
4. Time—when to buy and when to sell.

All three approaches are constantly comparing present action in a stock or group of stocks with past action in that stock or group and with present action in other stocks and other groups. As long as the present action is more or less in line with past patterns or the present action in other areas of the market, it holds little interest. However, let present action in a stock start to deviate or show some novel turn and it becomes a situation deserving the closest attention. It pays to watch the leader for a turn; and it is generally more profitable to ride with the leader on any move.

2

WHAT IS RECORDED ON THE TAPE

A more-or-less typical run on the tape on an average active day on the New York Stock Exchange might look like this:

CRI	HW	T		EK	PCT		FTR
$18\frac{3}{4}$	$13\frac{1}{8}$	$1000s137\frac{7}{8}$■$5s\frac{7}{8}$		$127\frac{3}{4}$	$5s8$■$2s8$■8		30

The one-, two- and three-letter listings on the top line are, of course, the stock symbols assigned each traded issue. The bottom line indicates the volume and price for each transaction. When a transaction is in the standard single-unit, 100-share lot (called a "sale"), no volume is indicated. However, when more shares are included in a single block, the volume is shown as "2s" (2 sales, or 200 shares), "3s" (300 shares), etc., to the left of the price. (But note that "1000s" means 1,000 shares, not 100,000.) Here is a translation of the above tape strip:

Number of Shares	Name of Stock	Price
100	Collins Radio	18¾
100	Howe Sound	13⅛
1,000	Amer. Tel. & Tel.	137⅞
500	Amer. Tel. & Tel.	137⅞
100	Eastman Kodak	127¾
500	Papercraft	8
200	Papercraft	8
100	Papercraft	8
100	Fruehauf	30

Note the three successive trades in Papercraft. These "bunched" trades do not necessarily have any special significance, since they may well reflect the mechanics of reporting and transmitting rather than a meaningful burst of activity. Bunching was far more prevalent in the days before the recording process was more fully mechanized.

Even with the high-speed ticker (900 characters per minute) introduced in the fall of 1964, the tape sometimes lags behind actual trading. When trading becomes especially active, the front digits are often left out after an announcement on the tape. Then the tape looks like this:

CAY	IT	SMC	REV	XRX	AVT	TX	LJ
$2s9\frac{5}{8}$	$9\frac{5}{8}\blacksquare 2s\frac{1}{2}$	$2s6\frac{7}{8}$	$7\frac{3}{4}$	$7s90$	$2s6\frac{7}{8}$	$4\frac{3}{8}$	$8\frac{3}{8}$

And the translation reads:

Number of Shares	Name of Stock	Price
200	Philip Carey Mfg.	29⅝
100	Intl. Tel. & Tel.	59⅝
200	Intl. Tel. & Tel.	59½
200	A. O. Smith	36⅞
100	Revlon	37¾
700	Xerox	90
200	Avnet Electronics	16⅞
100	Texaco	74⅜
100	Libby, McNeil & Libby	18⅜

In the past, volume, except for very big blocks, was also omitted after an announcement on the tape on very active trading days. Presumably, these omissions will become less frequent with the new "900 Ticker."

The stock ticker was first introduced in 1867. Over the last 100 years, the only essential change has been the constant trend toward greater speed in getting the records of each trade from the floor onto the tape. In 1965, a computer system, developed by IBM, was linked to the new 900 Ticker. With the aid of an optical scanner, this combination permits a trade to be transmitted from the floor in as little as half a second. Prior to this, each trade was noted on a slip of paper and transmitted by pneumatic tube to the ticker room. On a normal day there was about a three-minute lag between the time of the transaction and its appearance on the tape.

Though the stock ticker tape is "live" and closely reflects actual trading as it unfolds on the Exchange floor, it has one great drawback: the quotations it records are highly perishable. This is obviously true for the electronic board and, for all practical purposes, equally true for the yards and yards of paper tape. Some market operators like to take a more leisurely look at the details of a day's trading. For these operators, Francis Emory Fitch, Inc., 138 Pearl Street, New York 5, N. Y., makes available, for a subscription fee daily sheets which record in a permanent form all of the day's transactions. This is done by computers which sort the transactions stock by stock in sequence, showing the number of shares and the price of the trade. For example:

```
ACME STEEL CO              ADAMS MILLIS              ABBOTT LABS
    100   18 3/4               200    9 1/4              100  124 3/4
    100   18 3/4               100    9 1/4              300  124 1/4
    300   18 3/4               100    9 1/4              100  124
    100   18 3/4                                         100  123 3/4
    100   18 3/4
    100   18 3/4           ADDRESSOGRAPH
    100   18 3/4              1000   53 1/2             ABC CONSOLIDATED
                              300    53 3/4              100   13 5/8
                              600    53 1/2              100   13 5/8
ACME MARKETS                  300    53 1/2              600   13 1/2
    200   65 1/2               200    53 1/4              100   13 1/2
    100   65 3/4               200    53                 100   13 1/2
    100   65 1/2               300    52 7/8             100   13 1/2
    100   65 3/4               900    52 7/8             100   13 1/2
    100   66                   100    53
    100   65 1/2               100    53
                              100    52 7/8
ADAMS EXPRESS                  100    53 1/8             ACF INDUSTRIES
    500   25 5/8               100    53                 200   63 1/4
    100   25 3/4               300    52 3/4              100   63
    100   25 1/2               100    53 1/8             300   62 5/8
    100   25 5/8               100    53                 500   62 1/2
    100   25 5/8               330    53                 100   62 1/2
    200   25 5/8               300    53                 100   62 1/2
    100   25 1/2               100    52 3/4             100   62 1/2
    100   25 3/8               100    53 1/8             100   62 1/2
    300   25 3/8               100    53                 100   62 1/4
    100   25 3/8               100    53 1/8             100   62 3/4
    100   25 3/8               100    53                 100   62 3/4
```

Price and volume data in this form are especially useful to traders who wish to take special note of all of the big block transactions in a stock or a group of stocks. This reporting method is also handier for analysts wishing to reconstruct a day's action—by separating trades on upticks from those on downticks, for instance. There should be no essential difference between the amount of detail available on the actual tape and in the Fitch report, since both record every trade.

Few investors, however, have the time to follow or make use of this wealth of detail. Instead, most of them generally rely on daily or weekly summaries showing high, low, and closing prices and volume for the period covered.

-1965- Range			Sales in					Net
High	Low		100s	Open	High	Low	Close	Chg.
50	44⅛	Abbott Laboratories	22	47½	48½	47½	47⅞ +	⅛
23⅝	17⅛	ABC Consolidated	23	21⅝	22¼	21⅝	22¼ +	⅝
93	77⅝	ACF Industries	23	86	86¼	85⅝	86¼ +	⅝
73½	64	Acme Markets	6	68	68⅛	68	68⅛ +	⅛
28¾	27¼	Adams Express	18	28	28¼	28	28¼ +	¼
18¼	13⅛	Adams-Millis	18	15	15⅝	15	15⅝ +	⅝
55⅞	46½	Addressograph-Multigraph	81	48	48⅜	47¼	47⅝ −	½
33⅛	15⅝	Admiral Corporation	73	30¼	31⅛	30¼	31 +	¾

The actual tape, the daily market quotation sheets, and the published stock tables are the three chief sources of price and volume information available to the trader and investor. At first glance, they may appear to be a hopeless jumble, but in fact they provide the basic data for just about all of the elaborate technical tools that have been devised over the years for analyzing market trends and patterns.

3

USING AND ABUSING THE TAPE

From time to time, the tape has been blamed for the excesses of the market, and some reformers have even suggested that it be forbidden. But, the alternative—the somewhat artificial price quotations of the over-the-counter market—seems even less likely to serve the public interest.

Behind the criticism of the tape lies what may be called its "abuse" by pool managers and other trading syndicates of the past. These operations have often been described, but perhaps one of the best accounts was given by "an experienced manipulator" quoted in S. Nelson's *The A B C of Stock Speculation:*

> It is only fair to say that the public rarely sees value until it is most markedly demonstrated to them, and the demonstration comes generally at a pretty high price. It is easier for them, as experience shows, to believe a stock is cheap when it is relatively dear, than to believe it is cheap when it is more than cheap. A Stock Exchange operator or group of operators decides, we will say, that a certain stock is selling cheap—that is, below value. Value means, in Stock Exchange speculation, intrinsic value, plus future value, plus the additional Stock Exchange value. A large holder of the stock begins by going around to other large holders. Ownership is counted, and the outstanding stock in public hands is fairly estimated.

11

The first necessary detail is to "tie up" in a pool these known holdings, in order to prevent realizing sales by larger interests. If such large holdings cannot be kept off the market . . . [a] plan of accumulating the stock at low prices, before tying it up, is devised. This takes the form of manipulation within a certain range of prices. It may be assisted by natural stock market conditions, which encourage sales by outsiders at a sacrifice. Frequently persistent attacks on the stock by the people who wish to buy it are undertaken, which bring out miscellaneous public holdings, and which, if carried sufficiently far, dislodge even important inside holdings. To accomplish the decline, matched orders are frequently used, whereby the pool really sells to itself. Large offerings of the stock are also continually placed on the floor with no takers, resulting in the gradual lowering of commission-house selling limits, and the securing of cheap stock thereby.

The question of borrowing money is important. A pool can rarely do the whole thing with its own capital. It is assumed that the money market outlook favors a stable condition, for it is idle to suppose such operations would be conceived were conditions pointing otherwise. Money brokers have, of course, been employed by the house handling the pool, to borrow from the banks large amounts of time and short-time call money, termed "special loans," on which the collateral is largely to be the security in question, and on which a liberal rate is paid and liberal margins given.

The "publicity department" must also have been covered. Practically all important pool operators keep on hand this appendage to their work. The gossip affecting the stock must be printed, and this [publicity] is systematized to a degree few suspect. It is generally in charge of a man intimately connected with newspaper channels, covering every important city, if need be; this person receives a large compensation for distributing for circulation—when the managers of the pool see fit- items of news and gossip affecting the stock. The insiders being in the pool, every item of news is carefully bottled up and distributed only at what is thought to be the right time. The need for this will be apparent when it is observed that explanation must be made for advances, and excuse for declines, in all manipulated stocks. The fact that [the] insiders and the pool own the news, so to speak, and can thus discount its effect ahead of those who get it through publicity channels, involves a moral [question] which has often been the subject of Wall Street discussion.

The machinery of Stock Exchange work varies little. Orders are given to different sets of brokers from time to time to buy the stock, sometimes carefully and quietly, sometimes by openly and aggressively bidding for it; and vice-versa on the selling side. Rarely is one broker alone allowed to remain conspicuous on either side for any considerable length of time. All these transactions are "cleared" by the brokers filling the orders; that is, instead of [divulging] the names of their principals in the trades, they take in and deliver the stocks themselves, and then receive and deliver them from and to their principals.

Market conditions now being favorable to the deal, and emission of favorable news facts having resulted in public interest, the commission-house broker, who represents the "public," begins to be in receipt of many requests for opinion on the stock made active. The commission-house broker is a pretty good judge of the situation generally, and has spent his life studying values and watching manipulation. He thus assists in the operations by advising purchase. As a general rule, the advice falls flat, and few orders come out of it. But the pool continues; they are at present really buying stock and selling little. Some of these are actual trades, some are matched orders, but it is impossible, even for the brokers in the crowd, to tell which. . . . The result, however, is a marked stimulation of public interest, and commission-house buying orders begin. More news is published, and the deal becomes public talk.

When this condition is created, the stock is up several points, and the pool begins to figure on selling. The machinery of the publicity department is then worked to its utmost extent, and the following morning finds a general demand for the stock from all commission houses. This is the time when a "widespread" opening is figured on. Orders by the thousands are put in on the selling side, distributed to many brokers, with, of course, some buying orders also put in to a limited degree to "take it as offered" at the opening. The "high opening" is effected, and stock sold by balance sufficient to warrant pool support and renewed buying, after the overnight public orders have been filled. Then follows bold, aggressive buying by the pool in large quantities, aided by matched selling orders, and the volume of the business done attracts attention everywhere, and leads to enormous absorption by the public.

Given favorable conditions, the public buying thenceforward controls the market, and the pool places only supporting orders in the stock from time to time, when outside interest flags. This public buying will continue until it has carried the price so much beyond value that the pool can afford to liquidate freely. From then on, the operation proceeds to its profitable close; the various official, semi-official, and "inside" announcements of news and suggestions covering the outlook in the immediate and near future—[regarding] the value of the stock, dividends to be paid, bond conversions, new alliances, consolidations—are the only necessary machinery.

This was the general pattern. The important point for our purposes is the central role played by the tape in these manipulations by the pools early in this century. News was carefully controlled; often the brokers did not know how the buying and selling was going, and even the insiders were occasionally befuddled. The only thing that could not be masked was the action of the stock on the tape. Realizing this, the pool managers always had to take tape action into account and have plausible explanations for sudden shifts in price and volume.

Sensing that the pools had to surface occasionally on the tape, many professionals attempted to follow the moves of the pools by reading the price and volume sequences on the tape. In those days, pool managers were for hire, and many of these operators had characteristic methods of moving their stocks which often resulted in telltale patterns on the tape.

The general investing public attempted to follow these moves at a discreet distance. No less an authority than Charles H. Dow gave the public some practical advice on how to do so:

In a broad sense, trading on the Stock Exchange represents the operation of supply and demand as applied to securities. Ordinarily, however, a comparatively small part of the business is done by investors. The larger part is the outcome of professional trading and of the manipulation that is carried on by large interests to accomplish desired results.

Trading in stocks can ordinarily be divided into professional and public dealings. There is a great difference between the two. Professional trading includes manipulation and the operations of those who make trading in stocks a considerable part of their daily business. Trading by the public covers investment business and a form of dealing which is partly speculative and partly investment. The professional operator trades all the time. Public trading is variable and very uncertain.

The two extremes in the market are occupied by manipulators who either wish to buy or to sell in considerable quantity, and the public which, in the end, wishes to invest wisely. The manipulator, therefore, looks to the public to buy the stocks which he wishes to sell, or to sell those which he wishes to buy. A large proportion of all manipulation is aimed at the public, and professional traders are merely the middlemen who try to take profits out of the movements which manipulators appear to be trying to make.

Suppose that a syndicate finds itself with a profit in the form of $10,000,000 worth of stock. The way to convert this profit into cash is to sell the stock. The syndicate, therefore, makes an arrangement with some skilled manipulator, who undertakes to induce the public to buy this stock. He begins by seeing that the merits of the case are stated as fully and as widely as possible.

Whether the stock is intrinsically valuable and the enterprise sound or unsound makes a great difference as to the class of men [who] undertake the manipulation, but it makes but little difference as to the methods which are employed to secure public buying. In any event, the first thing is to have the property known about and talked about. The way to obtain this result is to have the stock do something which makes brokers and speculators and writers try to find out what is causing the movements which are recorded on the tape.

Manipulators in such cases usually tell friends that the stock in question is to be made active and advanced. This brings buying of a professional class, because it is understood that a deal of the magnitude proposed cannot be accomplished without sustaining the market for the stock for a considerable time during which trading in it will be comparatively safe. Manipulators know, furthermore, that one of the best ways of getting a stock talked about is to have people tell friends that they have made money by buying it. Accordingly, there is almost always money to be made with a minimum of risk in the early stages of such a campaign.

The manipulator must keep the stock active, buying and selling from ten to twenty thousand shares a day in order to keep traders confident of a market on which they can sell, if at any time they become alarmed. It is characteristic of the public to buy on advancing prices rather than on declining prices. A stock which is to be sold is therefore kept strong and advanced moderately if the general market will permit this to be done.

The larger the manipulation, the larger will be the volume of professional trading, and the greater the likelihood of the public taking an interest in the stock. Usually in such cases the public buying is at first small; then it becomes more confident; and finally there is full confidence and the stock is rapidly unloaded upon the public buying. Then the activity dies out, professional trading becomes less, and the public is satisfied or dissatisfied with its bargain, as the case may turn out.

This occurs to a greater or lesser extent in the market all the time. There is always some large interest which would like to have the public buy or sell, and manipulation is going on with that end in view. Large interests know that if the public can be induced to trade freely in stocks which are of unquestioned value, they can generally be led into other stocks; therefore, an attempt is often made to get the public into the market by advancing three or four leading stocks. If the public comes in, the market is widened. If the public does not come in, the manipulators discontinue their efforts to make a market after a few days and wait for a more opportune time.

The rule for the public ought to be essentially the rule which is followed by professional traders. When a stock is made active, consider it first with reference to its value. If it is intrinsically cheap, it can ordinarily be traded in as long as it is kept active. But it is generally wise to sell when activity ceases. If the stock is apparently above its value, a good deal more caution ought to be exercised about going in, and stop orders should be used to guard against severe drops.

Generally speaking, manipulation in a new property is for the purpose of selling; in an established property, bull manipulation is usually discounting some favorable news which insiders are holding back. Bear manipulation in perhaps eighty per cent of cases is the discounting of something which is unfavorable. In twenty per cent, perhaps, it is for the purpose of accumulating stock with reference to a succeeding rise.

As a whole, however, bear manipulation is founded on knowledge that the stock under treatment is intrinsically dear. It is not, as a rule, good judgment to buy stocks which are under attack until the attack ceases and there are indications of a rally on the short interest which may have been made by those who followed the decline.

Recognizing that only a small fraction of the average daily trading in a given stock could possibly represent investing (buying and holding for value), Charles Dow concluded that much depended on trading and manipulation, aimed at accomplishing some desired result. If properly understood, these manipulations could be used by the general investing public to realize profits.

Dow also felt that manipulation plays a role in general market moves. Perhaps this seems a somewhat surprising attitude for the man after whom the venerable Dow Theory is named, but here is Dow's analysis of the role of manipulation in general market trends:

The stock market alternates between periods of activity and periods of rest. Its periods of activity are usually started by manipulation and continued by a mixture of manipulation and public buying. Professional traders and the public usually try to follow the lead of some individual or clique which is apparently advancing some particular stock or stocks.

The main difference between manipulators and general traders is that the manipulator endeavors to take advantage of conditions which he thinks will exist in the future. He believes that the condition of money or change in the value of a particular stock or something else will cause a given security to be worth more three months hence than it is now. He buys stocks quietly and then advances the price slowly or rapidly, as the case may be, with the expectation that the public will take his stock off his hands when it sees what he saw at the beginning. Whether the public does this or refuses to do it determines the success of the campaign.

In a majority of cases, a well-sustained advance supported by large trading will bring enough outside buying to enable a manipulator to unload a substantial line of stock. The speculative public always buys on advances and seldom on declines, in which respect it differs from the investing public which buys on declines and sells on advances. One of the most skillful manipulators in Wall Street says that any stock possessing merit and having some influential [characteristic] to be made the basis of a campaign can be marketed at an advance in price, if the manipulating interest is willing to pay the cost of such a campaign, which would perhaps average $250,000.

This cost is chiefly applied to the creation of a market. The rules of the Stock Exchange do not permit A to tell B to buy stock from C at a given price, but [they do] not prohibit A from telling B to buy 10,000 shares of a given stock and at the same time telling C to sell 10,000 shares of the same stock. The results of such an operation would show that many brokers had participated in the trading, through a wish to take either the buying or the selling side, and that on the whole the market, although artificial in one sense, had been legitimate in the sense that anybody had a chance to step in and buy or sell at the price established.

A bull campaign in the market is a far bigger undertaking than a campaign in one stock, because many stocks have to be moved. On the other hand, it is sometimes easier because it invites cooperation from many sources, and sometimes a very small amount of encouragement in a stock is sufficient to induce its friends to do all that is required to promote an active speculation.

The general progress in a bull market is for the manipulating interest to take two or three prominent stocks, and, by making them active and higher, attract attention to the fact that a campaign has been started. It is customary to take stocks of the best class, in which there is a large investment interest and where the supply of floating stock liable to come on the market is known not to be large. This is why St. Paul is so often used as a leader, and why closely held stocks like Rock Island, Northwest and others of that class are frequently advanced materially at the beginning of a bull campaign.

After stocks of this kind have been put up from 5 to 10 points, it is customary to shift the trading to stocks of the middle class on the idea that the public will not buy where there [have] been very large advances or where prices are very high, but will buy the cheaper stocks, even if they are intrinsically dearer. After stocks of this kind have been carried up a few points, it is customary to take up stocks of still lower price. It was considered for many years that when manipulators moved Erie, the end of a period of rising prices was at hand, because Erie was regarded as of next to no value and putting it up was considered diversion of the public while other stocks were being sold.

In a prolonged bull campaign, after the manipulators have moved the low-priced stocks, they sometimes go back and move the others all over again, following the same order—the high-priced stocks first, stocks of the middle class next, and then the cheapest on the list.

With pools then all quite legal and constantly in the process of formation and liquidation, the great speculative eras of the past in the stock market, like 1896-1902 and the 1920's, were dominated by the men who were behind the tape. To understand what these men were doing, market traders read the tape. It wasn't necessary to guess whether "they" were buying; if "they" were really buying, it would show up soon enough on the tape.

Today, pools are illegal and some of the favorite methods used by pool operators are likewise illegal or at least hampered by the regulations. But big investors always find a way to speculate, and often this speculation attempts to push prices up or down. A single wealthy individual, quite without outside help, can accumulate a line of a given stock. If he invests several hundred thousand dollars, it seems safe to assume that he will do it in such a way as not to hurt the over-all value of his holdings. In acquiring a big position in a single stock, he may be said to be "manipulating" the stock, without doing too much violence to the meaning of the word.

Of course, this process will seldom be called manipulation. Most discussions of the market proceed today with a sanctimonious air, reflecting in part the regulatory climate in which the market now operates. But few can deny that big investors still attempt to influence stock prices; only the procedures have changed to fit the times. The implications of these new tape-reading approaches will be reviewed next.

4

WHO IS BEHIND THE TAPE TODAY

There are fewer tickers in operation now than there were in the late 1920's. On September 25, 1929, there were 9,707 stock tickers in operation; today there are approximately 3,800. This is rather surprising, especially when the rapid postwar growth in the number of brokerage offices and branches is taken into account. All of this would suggest that fewer traders today operate in such a way that they need the tape running constantly through their fingers.

Several factors make day-trading less popular now than in the 1920's. For one thing, the tax structure favors six-month holdings. Few big market operators find market profits made in a few hours or days as attractive, after taxes, as their fathers did in the 1920's. And the brokerage fees are higher now, making traders more reluctant to go in for a few points. Margins are higher, too, which also puts something of a damper on the fast in-and-outer.

As a result, the turnover rate—the number of shares traded as a percentage of average shares listed—has fallen to the lowest levels in history in the postwar years (see Table 1).

Of course, there are 7.9 billion shares listed now, as compared with 942.5 million in 1929; but, even so, total annual volume did not exceed that of 1929 until 1963. For the tape-reader, this means that the action time is now much slower. If a given move took only a few days back in the 1920's, it might stretch out over several weeks or even

20

TABLE 1

VOLUME, SHARES, AND TURNOVER RATE
(millions of shares)

Year	Reported Stock Volume	Average of Shares Listed	Per Cent Turnover	Year	Reported Stock Volume	Average of Shares Listed	Per Cent Turnover
1900	102.4	59.6	172%	1932	425.2	1,315.3	32%
1901	221.1	69.6	319	1933	654.8	1,302.6	50
1902	163.0	78.7	207	1934	323.8	1,299.4	25
1903	137.8	82.0	168	1935	381.6	1,311.6	29
1904	157.7	82.6	191	1936	496.0	1,339.1	37
1905	210.5	86.2	244	1937	409.5	1,386.2	30
1906	221.7	92.5	240	1938	297.5	1,418.1	21
1907	156.9	98.3	160	1939	262.0	1,429.8	18
1908	165.2	102.4	161	1940	207.6	1,445.1	14
1909	197.8	110.3	179	1941	170.6	1,459.0	12
1910	161.1	126.8	127	1942	125.7	1,466.9	9
1911	125.9	140.3	90	1943	278.7	1,479.9	19
1912	131.5	148.8	88	1944	263.1	1,490.8	18
1913	82.8	152.3	54	1945	377.6	1,542.2	24
1914*	47.4	154.8	31	1946	363.7	1,681.8	22
1915	172.5	155.8	111	1947	253.6	1,839.0	14
1916	232.6	160.2	145	1948	302.2	1,962.0	15
1917	184.6	179.7	103	1949	272.2	2,091.6	13
1918	143.3	193.9	74	1950	524.8	2,259.4	23
1919	318.3	208.0	153	1951	443.5	2,484.6	18
1920	227.6	251.1	91	1952	337.8	2,702.0	13
1921	172.8	292.7	59	1953	354.9	2,857.4	12
1922	260.9	337.2	77	1954	573.4	3,050.4	19
1923	236.5	393.2	60	1955	649.6	3,505.3	19
1924	284.0	424.8	67	1956	556.3	4,149.2	13
1925	459.7	462.5	99	1957	559.9	4,632.9	12
1926	451.9	538.6	84	1958	747.1	4,910.2	15
1927	581.7	620.3	94	1959	820.3	5,432.0	15
1928	930.9	706.2	132	1960	766.7	6,152.8	12
1929	1,124.8	942.5	119	1961	1,021.3	6,773.2	15
1930	810.6	1,212.2	67	1962	962.2	7,373.6	13
1931	576.8	1,307.8	44	1963	1,146.3	7,883.7	15
				1964	1,236.6	8,668.8	14

*July 31, 1914, Exchange closed due to pending outbreak of World War, and re-opened for trading in all stocks under restrictions December 15, 1914. Restrictions removed April 1, 1915.

months today. This would limit the need for minute-to-minute contact with the running tape.

Insider techniques also change. In recent years, an increasing share of trading has been done off the tape. There are the secondary offerings of big blocks, which are reported separately. In addition, there has been growth in the off-board trading of listed stocks. There are no firm figures on the exact size of this business, but estimates place it between 3 and 5 per cent of total annual volume. And there is the trading of inter-listed stocks on other exchanges around the country that is not recorded on the tape. All of this helps keep the tape quiet and permits big holders of an issue to be a little more secretive in their operations. However, even if all this leakage is allowed for, about 90 per cent of all transactions still take place on the Exchange and are duly recorded on the tape—a big enough sample to permit judgment in most cases.

With the pace of trading much slower than in the past, fast in-and-out trading based on tape-reading appears less promising than it was. If tape-reading has a contribution to make to the trader in today's market, it would appear to be as a method of spotting accumulation or distribution in an individual stock (or the market as a whole) that would influence price over a few weeks or months. These trends of accumulation or distribution are worth following only if they indicate "sponsorship" or informed buying and selling with some carrying power. Otherwise, what appear as "trends" may be merely random movements that could terminate as abruptly as they began and permit little profitable trading.

If pools are illegal, can it still be assumed that stocks have "sponsors" who are attempting to influence the ultimate outcome of a move? One of the prime requirements for sponsorship is sufficient funds to make your influence felt. In today's market there are three groups with adequate funds to influence stock prices: institutional investors, New York Stock Exchange (NYSE) member firms, and wealthy individuals. (See Chart 1).

Perhaps the most obvious difference between today's market and that of the 1920's is the growth in power and influence of the so-called institutional investors—mutual funds, pension funds, insurance companies. This group now controls about 20 per cent of all NYSE-listed stocks by value (see Table 2).

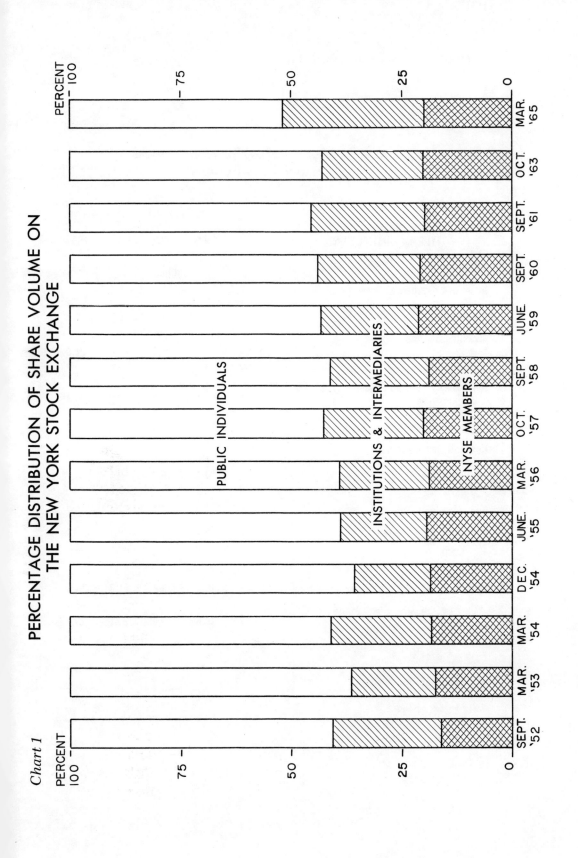

Chart 1

PERCENTAGE DISTRIBUTION OF SHARE VOLUME ON
THE NEW YORK STOCK EXCHANGE

TABLE 2

Estimated Holdings of NYSE Listed Stocks
by Financial Institutions

	YEAR END				
TYPE OF INSTITUTION	1949	1956	1962	1963	1964
	(Billions)				
Insurance Companies:					
Life	$1.1	$2.3	$4.1	$4.6	$5.3
Non-Life	1.7	4.5	7.1	8.2	9.2
Investment Companies:					
Open-End	1.4	7.1	15.4	18.6	21.8
Closed-End	1.6	4.0	5.3	5.7	6.5
Non-Insured Pension Funds:					
Corporate	0.5	5.3	17.9	22.6	27.4
Other Private	*	0.4	1.0	1.3	1.7
State and Local Government	*	0.2	0.8	1.0	1.3
Nonprofit Institutions:					
College & University Endowments	1.1	2.4	3.3	4.0	4.5
Foundations	1.1	4.1	6.7	8.1	9.2
Other	1.0	3.1	5.0	5.9	6.8
Common Trust Funds	*	1.0	1.7	2.4	2.7
Mutual Savings Banks	0.2	0.2	0.4	0.4	0.4
Total	$9.7	$34.6	$68.7	$82.8	$96.8
Market Value of All NYSE Listed Stocks	$76.3	$219.2	$345.8	$411.3	$474.3
Estimated Per Cent Held by all Institutions	12.7%	15.8%	19.9%	20.1%	20.4%

* Less than $50 million.

That these institutional investors have an important influence on day-to-day trading is quite evident from the annual NYSE surveys of stock volume by sources (see Chart 1). In recent years, institutional investors have been accounting for over 20 per cent of the volume on the survey days, with the reading in June, 1965 (the date of the last survey), being 31.4 per cent of daily volume.

On this same day in 1965, another monied group—NYSE member firms—accounted for 20.1 per cent of volume. This left 48.5 per cent to private individuals, but that group can hardly be lumped simply as the "public." About 41 per cent of trading by individuals was done by the highest income group—persons making $25,000 or more annually. People in this income bracket are most probably officers of companies or professionals who have access to some inside information about their own companies or their friends' companies. Even if they are merely playing their hunches, their incomes would suggest that they are able to exert some influence by their buying and selling. This $25,000-plus income group alone accounted for 19.9 per cent of total daily trading.

Together, these three groups, all financially able to provide some sponsorship in their chosen stocks, did 71.4 per cent of the trading on the survey day in June, 1965. It also seems a reasonable assumption that the members of any of these groups, once they had embarked on a program of buying or selling, would ride along at least some distance before giving up. This would provide a degree of sponsorship for the stocks of their choice.

The three groups have another trait in common: all employ the services of analysts, to a greater or lesser extent. As is well known, analysts looking at the same basic figures often come to somewhat similar conclusions. Some of the big operators will be influenced in their operations by what their analysts say, and this will tend to bring some unified action to bear in selected stocks. Inasmuch as fund managers, NYSE members, and wealthy individuals, including corporate insiders, come to think alike about a stock or the market, their collective action resembles, in many ways, the operations of pools in the 1920's.

These observations are not intended to suggest that there is something sinister afoot; they simply offer an explanation for the obvious fact that some stocks become trading favorites and have good "sponsorship" while others languish and are unable to attract a following. Ticker technique can provide helpful trading clues if it can cast some light on the methods used by the groups behind the ticker in today's market.

Part II presents the currently relevant portions of a handy manual of ticker technique written in the 1930's. The general rules set forth appear as valid today as when they were written and provide a broad framework for following the price-volume patterns on the ticker.

Part Two

GETTING SIGNALS OFF THE TAPE

EDITOR'S NOTE

Orline D. Foster compiled the original edition of *Ticker Technique* in 1935, and it has become one of the classic works in the field of tape-reading. Most of what the author said in 1935 is still applicable to to-day's market, but in some instances rules of trading and conditions have changed. Accordingly, some of the material in the original edition has been omitted, and some has been updated or expanded. In the latter case, the writings of other great tape-readers of the past have been drawn on to give fuller meaning to the original text.

While this additional material is being included in the interest of greater clarity, every effort has been made to keep it to the barest minimum. One of the most appealing features of the original edition of *Ticker Technique* was the fact that it brought together so much of the wisdom of tape-reading in such a small space. The aims of the present edition remain the same as those expressed in the original foreword:

> To the stock market every fluctuation on the ticker tape has its own meaning. The speed of the trading; the volume; the size of the blocks of stock; the fluctuation of the prices; the type of stocks in which the major trading is done—these are the mosaics from which he works out his pattern. By following the tape he knows whether it is a waiting market, a distributing market, a market of accumulation or whether indications point to a reversal.

> In the following pages it has been my intention to classify some of these signals that the average trader might study, and make use of them. No effort has been made to offer detailed information on individual moves, preference being given to making each statement concrete.

> *Ticker Technique* is intended as a handbook for traders, a book to be kept on every operator's desk.

5

PRICE—ITS LIMITATIONS AS AN INDICATOR

Prices are perhaps the most obvious feature of the ticker tape, at least to the unpracticed eye. Experienced tape-readers, of course, "see" many other things on the tape of equal, if not greater, importance. But the vast majority of investors are aware only of prices. And they "read" the tape to find out where prices are, not where they are going.

Yet today's prices can assist in forecasting tomorrow's. As price after price runs along the ticker, they begin to establish a pattern or trend—both for individual stocks and for the market as a whole.

Types of Trends

Market movements can be roughly divided into three types of fluctuations:

1. *The major trend.* A major trend or primary movement covers a period of months and has its source in fundamental economic conditions. Often lasting from eighteen months to two years, the major trend is part of the complete cycle which includes both the bull and bear markets and the intervening periods of accumulation and distribution.

2. *The intermediate swing.* An intermediate or secondary movement originates in market conditions but may be affected by fundamental factors. It may last for a period of weeks or even months and provides excellent opportunities for traders. Intermediate trends offer

30

time for a fair analysis of the market, as they are long enough to permit the trader to determine the direction of the move, take his position, secure a profit, and get in and out several times before the swing is over. In some markets these intermediate movements last as long as six months and can be gauged with reasonable accuracy. They offer a good opportunity for the conservative trader.

3. *The short turn.* Short turns or minor moves are purely technical, originate within the market itself, and are due to current news, market conditions or professional activity. Minor moves last only a few days—usually from two to five—although in exceptional circumstances minor moves have lasted from eight to fifteen days. However, the market rarely carries a minor movement further than five days at the most without a slight change, even though it may only last a few hours. Minor movements are hazardous. The trader must not be out of reach of the tape at any time during market hours for he must jump in and out quickly.

An accurate analysis of the trend is of vital importance to the market operator. Signals of change of trend, of intermediate reversals, of rallies and dips, are shown in the action of the ticker tape.

Change of Trend

Changes in major trends are caused by fundamental economic conditions. *No major trend continues indefinitely in either direction against the condition of the economic structure.*

Changes in trend are preceded by periods of irregularity. During these periods accumulation or distribution takes place. Stocks churn around within a narrow range but make no headway. Certain stocks make new highs (in a bull movement) or new lows (in a bear movement). The whole action of the market is erratic and highly puzzling to the onlooker.

Narrow trading ranges are an interruption of the trend and usually indicate a new movement, either major or minor. A narrow trading range occurring in a bull market near the top may signal the beginning of distribution. At a low place in a bear market, it is likely to indicate accumulation.

*Never trade in a market which does not show a definite trend. You
are just guessing.*

Conservative traders never buy or sell until the market itself indicates a change of trend. For this reason, permanent advances and declines get under way slowly. There is always plenty of time to buy and
sell even after a big move is under way, inasmuch as irregularity always precedes every major movement. The accumulation and distribution of large holdings require time.

Seasonal Factors in Trends

Trend changes often seem to follow a seasonal pattern. This is a
reflection of the seasonal nature of certain economic influences. For
example, in strong bull or bear markets, there is often a change in the
market trend at the *quarterly periods*, when dividend meetings occur

TABLE 3

Seasonal Factors in Trend Changes

Months to Watch for Trend Changes	Significant Events
January	Investment of funds; fiscal year dress-up; anticipated earnings statements may affect market
April	Quarterly earnings statements; usual slight reaction at income tax time (15th)
May	Last large break in an accumulating market often takes place
June-July	Six-months statements; fiscal year dress-up; income-tax time (June 15th); vacation period
August	Rising trend in expectation of fall upturn in business (latter part of month)
September-October	Fall business upturn; movement of grain; income-tax time (Sept 15th); quarterly earnings statements
December	Irregular market due to income-tax selling; often concludes with year-end rally

and statements of earnings are made. When times are normal, however, only slight fluctuations are likely at the quarters.

Turns in the major trend often come in spring or fall at these quarterly periods, when business shows a marked improvement or a phenomenal decline. Other seasonal factors are summarized in Table 3.

In a bull market, when conditions are improving, stocks often rise in anticipation of increased profits, stock dividends, or rights. In a bear market, when earnings are poor and dividends may be cut, the market may discount this news beforehand. In many cases professionals secure inside information and sell the market heavily before the bad news is made public.

Interpreting Price Signals

In using *Ticker Technique* to forecast trends, reliance on price action alone is somewhat risky, chiefly because prices are the most commonly used smoke screen for distribution, masking changes in trend, etc. During a period of irregularity, for instance, when the trend is turning down, professionals often bid up market leaders and liquidate other stocks under this cover. When a major turning point is near, watch the action of the lower-priced stocks. They may be even better indicators of a probable reversal of trend than the market leaders. The professional unloads easily because the public watches the leaders and analyzes prices instead of volume. This makes it possible to unload stocks all across the board if prices in the leading pivotal stocks are not allowed to break.

The general public is not trained to watch volume. It gauges the strength of the market by the prices of the leaders. When distribution has been accomplished and the leaders are allowed to break, the public is caught unaware, hurries to sell, and the break is on.

Higher prices attract the crowds. This considerably weakens the usefulness of price alone as an indicator. James R. Keene, a famous trader of the past, once remarked: "The way to sell stocks to the public is to manipulate them to the highest point possible and sell them on the way down." Despite the obvious pitfalls in following price, it can serve as a useful clue in certain situations. Here are some guides to interpreting price action:

1. *Watch prices at new highs.* When a stock breaks through all

recent highs and advances into new territory, the start of an important move is indicated.

2. *Be wary of sharp price rises.* Never follow sharp rallies where a stock jumps half a point or more between sales and where the pace is swift. This shows short covering, not a change of trend. The rally will expend itself soon and the technical structure of the market will be weakened. This means lower prices, at least temporarily.

3. *Don't follow a wild opening.* Never jump in and cover shorts at a wild opening. Such markets tend to stabilize after 10:30. *When the highs of the day are registered during the first hour the market advance is technical and temporary.*

4. Price is a poor guide at bull market tops. *When prices advance rapidly at the top of a bull market or after a strong upward move and the volume increases, look out for a down turn.* This is the signal of distribution.

5. Price can help signal a bottom in a bear market. *When prices fall rapidly at the bottom of a bear market accompanied by heavy volume and when new lows are being made in important stocks,* it is an indication that the period of accumulation for the upward move is nearly over. *All shorts should be covered.*

6. *Watch for significant price patterns at bottom.* A trading area at the bottom of a decline is often a zone of accumulation and the next move is upward.

When a stock remains within a narrow range for a period of weeks and then moves into new high territory, distribution is over and a new move is under way.

When the price of a stock continues to bump at a given base, accumulation is indicated.

When stocks refuse to retreat perceptibly under professional pressure after a major decline and when volume is light, indications are that the market is at bottom.

When the market fails to decline on bad news after a long downtrend, the indication is for a sold-out condition and a probable rally.

It is reasonably safe to go along for at least a technical rally under such conditions. Watch the market. Follow up your gains with stops and play for a possible turn in the trend.

Stocks which go into new low territory on a sharp dip are often a buy for a few points upturn when approximate bottoms have been reached. When a stock makes a new low either for the year or for that individual move, it is usually safe (if it is an important stock) to buy it for a quick, sharp rally.

7. *Don't be fooled by price smoke screens.* Always be suspicious of a signal based on price alone. A run-up in a stock is *not* a sufficient reason for buying it; nor does a sharp sell-off necessarily make it a bargain.

For example, a large block of stock may be sold under the bid price. When this is followed by the sale of several small blocks at prices above the last sale, watch the market. It may be that the stock is being bid up in small lots to create a market at a better price so that another large block can be unloaded.

Another price maneuver is sometimes seen when a large operator wishes to accumulate stock. He sells a large block and then, after attracting attention, buys small parcels at lower figures to indicate there is plenty to be had. When the public begins to sell and the price drops, he buys another large block.

Some of the pitfalls can be avoided by becoming familiar with the patterns of individual issues. When you study the movement of a stock, note the number of points it covers in its moves: each stock has its own distinct behavior pattern. For example, when a certain stock breaks 88 it will go to 83, or if it starts up from 88 it will go to 93. Analysis of a stock will often make it possible to discern very definite cyclical moves of say, 15 points or 22 points.

The surest way to avoid being misled by price is to supplement it with an analysis of other factors, especially volume. In all cases it is necessary to determine whether the demand for stocks is greater than the supply. If it is, prices will advance; otherwise they will decline. The volume reflects the relative positions of supply and demand. The price shows the *value* of the volume.

6

VOLUME—WHY TAPE-READERS THINK
IT IS IMPORTANT

Trading volume—for the market as a whole and for individual stocks—is given a place of extreme importance in the trading methods of most of the leading tape-readers of the past. Yet, it continues to be one of the most neglected of the indications available from the tape. While the public watches the price, the volume figures can give away the insiders' moves.

If you doubt the importance of volume, look at it this way: volume is the measure of the money moving into or out of a stock. A two-point rise on 10,000 volume comes to $20,000, but a two-point rise in the same stock on 25,000 volume represents $50,000. The fact that this added buying power has been attracted to the stock should give a prospective purchaser more confidence in its ability not only to make the two points, but carry even higher. Thus, volume helps locate buying power—or selling pressure. And for that reason, volume is a more important indicator than price.

Volume and General Market Conditions

In order to understand the significance of volume, it is first necessary to relate it to the general state of the market at a given time:

In bull markets, when high volume appears at the top of a move-

37

ment with no increase in prices, it indicates that distribution is taking place.

In bear markets, when high volume appears at the bottom and prices do not fall off appreciably, it signifies that accumulation has been completed and the turn is near. Sound investors buy at the bottom, before the public comes back into the market; so accumulation always takes place on low volume.

In a dull market, the direction the averages take on increased volume should, under normal technical conditions, indicate the direction of the next move.

In irregular markets, volume is especially significant. Big volume on higher prices indicates demand. Big volume on lower prices indicates distribution.

When a market reverses itself on high volume, that usually means a definite change of trend.

Volume in individual stocks is often worth watching, not only for trends in these stocks themselves, but also for clues to the general market trend. In a bear market, for instance, selective volume is more important than general volume. When selling volume in popular stocks dries up, the market is about sold out.

Accumulation and Distribution

Volume offers the most reliable guide to accumulation and distribution of stocks.

Accumulation is the buying of stocks for the investor (for box account) or for the trader. It shows in both large and small blocks and also *denotes* an upturn. Real accumulation takes place in markets of *small volume.*

When volume increases on the upside in steady, orderly fashion, it indicates investment buying, especially if it is over a broad front or in preferred and investment issues.

Distribution is customarily preceded by great irregularity, a wide range of prices in the popular stocks, and a rushing up of the favorites into new high ground. This, together with increased volume, is a sure sign that large holders are distributing stock.

A sharp drop with a listless comeback is a sign of distribution, as is high volume following a swift run-up in prices.

Group distribution is made on high volume. The stock is distributed *on the way up*. When a stock hesitates on its high, with high volume, group distribution has probably been almost completed.

Irregularity often occurs during the marking-up process due to the fact that, if the stock's price appears to slip too low during distribution, the group is compelled to buy more stock which it marks up and redistributes.

A rapid rush of prices toward new highs, with special stocks making new highs for the move and accompanied by heavy volume, is a warning signal of distribution.

Occasionally distribution turns into something considerably more disorderly—distress selling, liquidation, or short selling.

Distress selling. When popular trading stocks are heavily sold, it usually indicates distress selling of margined stocks, although it could also be short selling. The time of day is significant: distress selling is generally done between noon and one o'clock, or between two and three.

Short selling. When large blocks of stock come out and prices fall rapidly, this signifies short selling. Irregularity of both price and volume, with prices dropping a quarter or half a point between sales, indicates short selling.

Margin and short selling are swift, and prices drop rapidly between sales. Forced selling and short selling orders go in "at market," which sends prices off quickly. This type of selling is easily detected because it affects the highly speculative line of stocks generally carried on margin. These are also the favorites for short sales.

Short covering is indicated when volume increases on the upside in rapid fashion, stocks jump a quarter, a half, or even a point between sales, and the speculative stocks begin to come out in long strings on the tape. *The result will be a weaker market after the excitement is over.* When the shorts have been driven out, the market is weakened technically because it has lost the buying power which lay underneath. This is especially true in a bear market where the shorts offer the main buying power. A short interest always provides a cushion of buying underneath the market, for shorts will cover on all sharp dips.

In contrast with short covering, good buying is never spasmodic.

A short position is a temporary thing. Any good news may make it untenable. When you see stocks rushing upward on volume, *wait* unless you have been able to buy right at the start of the move. Prices will drop again.

Liquidation is more persistent than margin selling and covers a broader front. It affects investment as well as speculative stocks. It is evidenced by a steady decline in prices and continual offerings which the market finds increasingly difficult to absorb. Prices drift steadily lower with each sale. This is in contrast to short selling, where the selling is more spasmodic, with wider gaps between sales.

As a rule, high-volume or "climax" selling puts a final end to a liquidating market. Sometimes, however, the liquidation comes slowly over a long period, taking the place of climax selling.

Watch the stocks which are being sold on a downtrend. When investment stocks, either preferred or common, begin to come out on the market in large blocks and prices drift steadily lower, it is liquidation.

Drastic liquidation is in most cases followed by a rapid advance. Sometimes the advance is merely short covering. If liquidation continues until it runs into climax selling, it is followed by a change in the market trend.

Persistent pressure on the market with no apparent comeback indicates intelligent selling for some definite reason. Sell with it and do not go back into the market until you see important buying.

How to Follow Volume

Some useful general rules for following volume are given below:

1. *Daily volume.* A market which is down in the morning and up in the afternoon is often a signal of accumulation and frequently indicates that a reversal is near. When prices drift along all day, there is usually a turn at the close.

2. *Spotting a reversal.* A trend which struggles hard but gets nowhere usually precedes a sudden reversal. Heavy volume at the end of any move is likewise a sign of some kind of turn.

3. *When high volume is bullish.* Volume increases during an advance and only light volume on the setbacks show that the demand is greater than the supply and indicate a resumption of the advance.

Climax selling at the bottom of a bear market is also the natural signal for an upturn.

4. *When high volume is bearish.* If volume increases on the downside, it usually indicates lower prices. When a stock breaks through a support level on volume, it is a signal of eventual lower prices, even if the stock first has a "pullback." Decreasing prices with increased volume always indicate a lower trend.

When volume increases at the *top* of a rally or an advance, and prices churn around with no appreciable gains, it indicates a turning point.

When a stock reverses its action after making a new high and volume increases, it is headed toward lower levels.

If a market declines after a stabilization period and the volume increases on the decline, lower prices are in order.

Climax selling occurs when operators begin to grow nervous over conditions and dump their securities on the market. Such selling is more marked at the end of a bull market than at the close of a bear market, as it is caused by the public dumping stocks.

5. *When low volume is bullish.* If large blocks appear at steadily increasing prices, watch the market when it slows down to smaller lots. If little weakness is shown and few large blocks change hands at lower prices, the trend is upward.

Decreasing volume on lower prices is a positive signal. If volume decreases when new lows are being made, the buying is better than the selling.

When turns in the market do not start from a selling climax, they make their base during general irregularity and under cover of the highly individual movements of selective stocks. Indications of support come from shrinkage of volume on the downside.

When a change of trend takes place on light volume, it is usually preceded by a period of dullness. Selling dries up and sporadic waves of selling die of inertia. Feeble rallies set in and, after a struggling upward movement, the market reacts. Blocks are small, the general volume is light, and the market creeps upward with an effort until it gets public support, when larger blocks make their appearance.

When volume diminishes on the downside, it indicates an end to liquidation, and if bear drives are diminishing, an upturn naturally follows.

In an irregular market where stocks run up and down, when they have greater volume on the upside and volume diminishes on lower prices, an upturn is indicated.

When a stock penetrates long-established resistance points on high volume during a violent move, it may mean higher prices; but temporarily the technical strength of the market has been exhausted during the effort and a slight reaction must follow. This offers an opportunity for buying. The same rule holds true when new lows are made. The market becomes oversold, exhausted on the downside, and a rally is in order.

During an advance in the market, when stocks rally sharply on increasing volume and then slow down, watch the volume. If it diminishes slightly, even though prices sag, it indicates little stock for sale; otherwise it would sell off sharply. If prices decline on small volume, the advance may be resumed.

6. *When low volume is bearish.* When there has been an intermediate recovery during a major bear movement and resistance levels have been formed, a decrease in volume indicates that buying power has been exhausted and the downward movement will be resumed.

A shrinkage of volume on an upward move always indicates lower prices. When the advance appears to grow tired or struggles to go higher and then dies at the top, this signifies lack of demand and the end of the rally.

When stocks creep forward on light volume and selling orders are also light, chart formations show a rounding top or "round" turn. (See Chapter II). This is usually followed by high volume on the downside.

7

BREADTH—HOW TO TELL IF YOUR STOCKS ARE KEEPING UP

The market and its leaders usually move "in gear." When they part company—start to diverge—this is often an important signal. If a particular stock starts to run up while the market as a whole is sluggish or in a downtrend, the stock deserves careful consideration as a possible buy candidate for an upturn. On the other hand, if a stock suddenly breaks down while the market as a whole still shows strength, this signals caution and may mean sell. Watching a stock in relation to the rest of the market can often yield important clues to selecting and selling.

Stocks move on the technical condition of the market. Their value to you is predicated on the price at which they may be bought and sold. For this reason, fundamental values do not count in trading as they do in investment, but the wise trader deals only in *sound* stocks. All sound stocks are not necessarily good trading stocks, but certain good trading stocks are also sound. Select your stocks carefully. If you get "hung up" in a position, you will be happier when you know you are holding a good stock.

Selecting Stocks for New Buying

Check the market list each day. Stocks that show larger volume are active and likely to prove leaders.

43

Watch the stocks which rise fastest in periods of accumulation on high volume. Such action indicates a scarcity of stock.

Watch stock which rallies on small volume. This also indicates that there is little for sale.

Never deal in a stock which lacks good sponsorship or good backing. It should also be a popular favorite if you are using it for trading.

Trading in Issues with Small Floating Supplies

Issues which are small or which have only a small floating supply move the most rapidly, as the market is thin, but they also make trading hazardous. Be guided by your capacity for trading and your ability to handle a difficult situation.

Trying to trade in issues with small floating supplies can often prove dangerous. It takes less work to lift an issue with 500,000 shares actively traded than an issue with 5 million shares in floating supply; many of the mystery issues that suddenly skyrocket for no apparent reason prove to be "thin issues." While these issues occasionally show quick profits, they also show sudden drops as well. Most traders will usually do better with issues where the floating supplies are large enough to permit more moderate swings in the price. If you do see some merit in a thin issue, the best practice would seem to be to accumulate it without attempting to buy right on the breakout, and to sell it at some point in the wild ride if it comes.

Study the volume of sales in the stock in which you are trading whenever the market makes important tops and bottoms, and take into consideration the floating supply of that stock in determining whether the buying is better than the selling.

Watching Other Stocks for Clues to Yours

To determine the position of the market, watch the individual volume of representative stocks as well as those in which you are trading. When a large block of stock changes hands, follow up the next sale. If the price is lower, it indicates selling, especially if large blocks follow at still lower prices. If the prices continue gradually higher, it indicates good buying.

When large blocks come out at irregular prices, first a little lower, then a little higher, it may mean either group distribution or short selling under cover of some buying. Follow prices and volume closely until a definite trend is established.

When large blocks of a stock continue to come out at the same price, check on the large blocks in other stocks of the same industry to help determine the trend.

Also, always watch the general market closely and determine whether it is picking up activity on the downside or is moving higher. When the general list does not follow a market leader in a rally, it may be that other stocks are being sold under cover of the leader's activity.

Highly selective movements in stocks are characteristic of the tops and bottoms of broad swings.

8

TIMING—WHEN TO BUY AND
HOW SOON TO SELL

Timing can make quite a difference in the potential profitability of any market move. Good stocks usually make their moves more quickly in an active market. Long-run moves are, of course, influenced by fundamental conditions. But shorter-run patterns in stocks and the market as a whole are greatly influenced by technical considerations— and the action of professionals—which can be spotted by a careful reading of the tape.

Your aim should be to follow the public part-way in all major movements but to try to precede it in buying or selling. Remember, public participation is always greatest at tops and bottoms.

Spotting Uptrends from the Tape

When you think the market is close to an upturn, watch for evidence of an oversold condition. Notice the volume on different trades at their low price. If it is light, and if the market has been heavily sold for some time and prices all along the line are either making or approaching record lows, the market is probably sold out.

Other indications of a sold-out condition and change of trend are "double bottoms" in the prices of stocks and a continued drop in brokers' loans. Double bottoms (see Chapter 11) indicate that there is little stock to be had. The drop in brokers' loans shows that margin accounts are low and that stocks are in strong hands and have been bought outright. (Stock bought outright has usually been purchased for investment accounts and is not dislodged by ordinary market shakeouts.)

When stocks sell into new ground on markedly increased volume and then close plus for the day, it indicates at least a technical rally. When the decline has covered a long period and the selling is in the form of a selling climax, it indicates bottom and a probable change of trend.

A turn can also come on comparatively light volume without a selling climax when there has been serious liquidation, brokers' loans are very low, prices are near the bottom, and the public is heavily short. Instead of the selling climax, the market struggles irregularly at its low. Sporadic rallies are followed by small reactions. The market goes up and down on a broad bottom. Selling dries up on the dips, and the market begins to stabilize for an advance.

The following are some of the important tape signals that usually precede an upturn: when—

—turnover diminishes at the bottom of a bear market.

—price fluctuations in stocks continue within a narrow range, and selling ceases to come into the market.

—bear drives fail to carry stocks to new lows and there is evidence of support.

—there appears to be buying in preferred stocks.

—the averages begin to show more plus signs each week than minus signs.

—there is unusual weakness all through the morning, but stocks usually rally before the close.

—most of the day's gain is held to the close, the advance has not been too rapid, and the volume of sales is normal.

—there has been pressure all morning but the leaders are still above the lows of the previous day.

—each resistance level is a little higher than the previous one, establishing an upward trend line (known as "ascending bottom") (see Chapter 11).

—80 per cent or more of the stocks which show changes for the day are minus for three days in succession, you can expect at least a technical rally. (A normal technical rally in a bear market retraces one-third to one-half of the distance between the high and low points of the previous downward move.)

—most of the activity is crowded into the first or last hour, the move is rarely important. It is unusually a crowding of the shorts or short covering. This is especially true before a long holiday weekend.

Spotting Downtrends from the Tape

When the market is approaching the top of a movement, rallies are sporadic and fail to make new highs. On each upward move the main line of stocks falls a little below its previous high figure. The market struggles to advance, but fails. Certain popular stocks are driven to new highs but fall back again. Buying dries up and selling begins as operators see they cannot obtain higher prices. Demand is light. Some of the popular stocks are driven to sensational highs; under cover of this irregularity, distribution and short selling are going on.

Large blocks of stock begin coming out on the market and prices slip rapidly as there are fewer buyers. Under some circumstances, the market rallies again and often establishes what is known to chart readers as a "broad top." Where climax selling does not appear at this point, the market sags and selling comes on gradually increasing volume. Distribution is taking place and the downward trend has begun.

After the period of irregularity, the actual change of trend is climax selling. Large blocks of stock appear on the tape, volume increases rapidly, and the tape falls behind. Distribution is always more climactic than ordinary selling. At the first sign of a break, the public becomes alarmed, professionals scurry to safeguard their profits, and a wild scramble ensues.

When prices break widely between sales, and at the close there are losses of from six to eight points in medium-priced issues, this indicates distress selling and the probable approach of a climax. Climax selling is more likely to appear when the market is of a speculative character than when it is evenly divided between the liquidation of outright interests and margin selling.

Gold mining stocks often rise in a bear market because of the increased purchasing power of gold in times of depression.

Part Three

THREE BASIC APPROACHES
TO USING
TICKER TECHNIQUE

9

TRANSACTION-BY-TRANSACTION APPROACH TO TAPE-READING

by Herbert Liesner*

Following the live tape can be fascinating. Admittedly, you have to have a little of the expert's special knowledge to keep your interest up. For instance, you have to be familiar with a few of the stock symbols, or else the tape will look like a frieze out of an Egyptian tomb. But commit a few of these to memory, and the effects can be hypnotic.

Occasionally, especially when the trading gets spirited, it all may strike you as a little artificial. You are impatiently waiting for the next trade in C, and all that comes is an endless string of B, UTP, ROH, FLR, and CWE. In some ways, it is like the old remote, play-by-play baseball broadcasts on the local radio station when the home team was on the circuit. You know that something very crucial may be happening at this exact moment, but all you can do is wait for the tape to grind it out. If you are fully aware of the meaning of the tape, however, when the signal comes, it doesn't take the histrionics of a studio announcer to give it heightened meaning. It's all there neat and tidy— so many shares at a very precise price.

---

*Herbert Liesner, market analyst, investor and trader, is a veteran of 25 years of tape-reading, currently on the technical staff of *Indicator Digest*.

But reading the live tape has one very important drawback—it requires great concentration. In fact, the ideal set-up would be to have an office of your own, with a ticker-tape rather than a translux. This way you could let the tape store up its data while you ease your eyes for a time, attempt any telephone calls you might want to make, or post some of the figures you have already noted. Constant interruptions, which are prevalent in the average office, are among the worst hazards in watching a tape.

There's another advantage the ticker-tape has over the translux. One means of reading the tape is by the sound of the ticker. Just as the trading floor of the stock exchanges gives off characteristic sounds as the pace of trading quickens and then falls away, the speed or hum of the ticker-tape can tell you about the relative activity.

It usually takes some homework to get the most out of the live tape. On even the dullest trading day, there are literally thousands of individual transactions recorded on the tape. Obviously, you can't watch everything at once; so you have to be selective and decide in advance just where you are going to concentrate your attention.

Regardless of the stocks in which you have a position or might be interested in trading, it always pays to keep an eye on a few of the Dow Industrials, some of the most active stocks, and a sampling of the stocks that have been giving leadership to the market in recent weeks. If you plan to drop into your broker's and watch the tape, check your morning newspaper for the fifteen most active stocks from yesterday's trading.

It would also be helpful to check the charts on six or eight of these activity leaders and locate possible breakout points or breakdown points, if time permits, before looking at the tape. This will give you some feel for these stocks. Often, trends in the activity leaders during the day will give some clues to the trend of the market for the day.

Market leaders or "key" stocks are also important for spotting general market trends. Every market has some groups or specialties that seem to overpower the market and dominate the trading. In 1963-64, for instance, they were issues such as Xerox, Control Data, Chrysler, and, of course, the Airlines.

Here's how these market leaders can point to changes in the general market trend:

A market may go for a time (usually three to seven or eight days) under the leadership of a few particular groups or individual stocks; but, by about the sixth or seventh day, you may find that new specialties or new groups are assuming leadership. The issues which formerly led the advance are now faltering.

This, of course, can be due simply to the fact that the leaders have already had a pretty big advance and are entitled to a rest. Therefore, the first time this happens, don't put too much weight on the hesitation.

But, let the market continue advancing for another two or three weeks, while the former front-runners go into a trading range, with new specialties or new groups taking over the leadership day to day, and you should begin to proceed with caution.

You should be especially watchful if the leadership from day to day, or even from hour to hour, begins to rotate very rapidly. When this happens, after an advancing market, it usually signals a forthcoming reaction.

The same—in reverse, of course—would hold true in a declining market. That is, the leadership on the downside begins to change, new specialties start to fall off, new groups weaken. Suddenly, there is some very rapid switching from stock to stock or group to group—in some cases these rotating sinking-spells lasting as little as fifteen minutes in a single spot. Then, we know there will be a rally before too long.

Times to Keep a Close Check on the Tape

In the morning, when the ticker is turned on, the first thing that hits your eye is, of course, "Market Open." If you are able to watch the opening, there are several things to look for in particular.

It is important to watch the first stocks that appear on the tape. Very often, if they are in strong demand, buyers will not wait until the market has been open too long to start snapping them up; so keep your eye on stocks that are active around the opening, particularly if any of them open with a block. And it is essential to watch the ensuing trades in these early activity leaders and notice whether the ticks are up or down.

At the opening, you should also watch for either a continuation of or a break with the day-before pattern. If the market has closed mixed and opens mixed, it doesn't help you very much. But, if for two days running the market has closed at the top and opens the following morning a shade higher, then you can assume that the trend will continue in that direction.

By the same token, if the market has closed at the bottom for two consecutive days, shading the following morning (you can ignore an unchanged opening) then you can expect further decline. When shading to the lower side appears on the third morning, it usually pays to sell on the first minor rally. In a generally advancing market, the first dip can be used as a buying point.

When you watch the opening, check on some of yesterday's fifteen most active issues, stocks that have been in leadership recently, or any other representative cross-section of trading stocks. See if these stocks are opening higher or lower, for how a majority of them opened offers you a usually reliable clue to the trend of the market.

Some tape-readers also keep tabs on the stocks making new highs in an advancing market, or the stocks making new lows in a declining market. These are available each morning in many newspapers, and their openings can give you hints about the trend of the market.

At this point however, a word of caution is in order. Do not try to watch too many stocks. Especially at first, you should concentrate on no more than about half a dozen stocks—about as many as you will ever be able to follow in practice for trading purposes. You can keep your eye on the others occasionally.

Often it pays to have a brief glance at the whole collection of stocks running along the tape. If you watch a few feet at random, you may notice a little activity in a particular issue, perhaps one that you were planning to watch. It might have been trading 2500 to 3500 shares per day, nothing to make you want to do anything. But one day you notice that the volume has picked up to 5000 or 6000.

Then, you note that on upticks you are no longer getting 200 or 300 shares, but 500 or 1000 shares. And the stock may already have advanced two or three points.

Assuming that this stock is selling at somewhere between 35 and 50 and is still in an accumulation area, then the chances are that it will have at least a one-and-a-half- to two-point reaction before resuming bidding. By "resuming bidding," I mean that those who are accumulating the stock will once more raise their bids.

Occasionally, too, you will see, during a bull move, that a stock has a reaction and then suddenly a block of 5,000, 10,000 or 15,000 or more shares will appear on the tape. This may represent profit-taking by large holders who feel that the immediate move has reached its maximum, and who may be switching to another stock which is breaking out into activity.

Of course, it can also represent catching a stop-loss order, in which event, the stock thereafter would not sell any lower than at the block price. In most cases thereafter the stock will rebound a point or a point and a half, then it may level off before it resumes its advance.

It generally pays to watch the market very closely for the first half hour. If the market has closed strong the day before and opens strong, watch a fair representation of stocks across the board: if they continue to post highs at the end of the first half hour, the trend will most likely continue strong.

On the other hand, if by the end of the first half hour, stocks generally are not following the strong opening and are not making new highs, then it is probably wise to sell those stocks that have been active in the advance for moderate profits.

Another important time to watch the market is about 2:55 p.m. If the market from about 1:30 on has been without any definite trend, around 2:55 the floor traders will either cover shorts or go out of long stock. Therefore, the trend that sets in from about 2:55 generally will carry through to the close.

Sometimes you will hear the expression: "the rally started too early." This would generally hold true when the market has declined and there's a rallying phase. Or it may be that it's been quiet most of the day, with a rally effort getting underway at about 2:15 or 2:20. Under these circumstances, it is unreasonable to expect that there would be enough buying power to carry the market through to the close. Therefore, it is important to watch the market at about 2:55 for any signs of reactionary tendencies. If these begin to show by 3 o'clock, it is likely that this market will sell off to the close.

There are other habits of the market which are related to the clock. In a bull move, a reaction may often start between 12:30 and 1:30, because floor traders know that people who have no other time to watch the market except on their lunch hour can be shaken out by a reaction. In a rally during a bear phase, the market may be strong from 12:30 to 1:30 for the lunch-hour crowd, to keep up their enthusiasm and to get them to hold on to their long stock.

If the market is in an advancing phase, sometimes you will note that about five minutes (or even three minutes) before the close there will be a little dip. This could represent selling by so-called daylighters or day traders; and if the movement is strong—that is, to the upside— as soon as these day traders have sold out their stock, issues will snap right back and close higher than the dip level. By the same token in a declining market, you may get a little rally three to five minutes before the close which would represent short covering by day traders. As soon as this covering has been completed, stocks will again ease off towards the final close.

Days of the Week and the Tape

The habits of the bear market are fairly persistent. As a rule, bear markets decline into Monday morning, sometimes even Tuesday. Then they will rally until late Wednesday afternoon or Thursday at about one or two o'clock. Then the decline will be resumed into the following Monday or Tuesday.

In pre-war bull markets, large pool operators generated reactions after 2:15 p.m. on Thursdays in order to pick up stock. Since there was no interest charge on stock bought from 2:15 Thursday through Monday morning, you can imagine the savings this represented. These reactions generally wound up Saturday morning about 11 o'clock, and then the advance was resumed.

I believe that this old habit is almost built into the modern market; and in bull moves at the present time there still appears to be a persistent habit of Thursday afternoon reactions. Of course, these now will probably carry only into Friday morning or mid-day, at which time any advance will be resumed.

Special Tape Signals to Watch for

A market in which to be cautious: one that shows general dullness during a reaction, with a sudden move by two or three stocks to break out on volume and advance one-and-a-half or two points. If the rest of the list refuses to follow, you can be certain a general market reaction will shortly ensue.

A market that can highlight bargains: one that is in a reactionary phase, with the particular stocks you are interested in showing great resistance to any decline. Of course, this holds true for any stocks you might notice that are showing persistent tendencies to buck the decline of the general list. As soon as selling pressure lets up on the general list, these special stocks which have shown resistance are the best ones to buy.

In a normal market the particular stock you are following, having closed reasonably strong will sometimes open off one or two points. Or, it may have been somewhat weak and open up one or two points. This is generally done to test the market. If the stock in the upward move is marked down at the opening and no stock comes in following the downward opening, it indicates that there is very little stock in supply and this is a good point at which to buy. Where the stock has been weak and has opened up one or two points, the market is being tested to see whether the shorts will run for cover or whether buyers can be brought in. If the stock makes little advance after the opening, it generally is a good sale.

Reaction to the News

Another important factor in tape-reading is to watch the reaction to news items. If a stock has been advancing, and a good earnings statement is put out or a bullish statement is issued by one of the company officers but the stock does not advance, this would indicate a weak technical position of the individual stock. You are likely to get a reaction.

By the same token in a declining market, if a poor earnings statement or a bearish statement by a service or company officer is published and the stock refuses to go down, it generally will be a buy for at least a good rally.

However, if there is a movement down, and you can find no apparent cause, and the volume increases, this would indicate a very weak technical position. Of course, this could be just profit-taking by weak holders. You would have to watch at this point to see whether the former support points are holding.

If there has been an extended rise—either by the market as a whole or by the individual stock you are watching—the first reaction nearly always takes place on a day of heavy profit-taking. It is important to watch the low of the reaction on a day of this sort, or possibly the next day, because this will become your main support area and should not be broken if the stock is going to resume its climb or make new highs any time soon.

In a bull market, a dip that does not break its supports is generally called a healthy reaction. But if it does break its supports after an extended advance, it may well presage a very heavy decline. Generally, also, you can judge the declines by the extent of the reaction. If it is not more than about one-third or one half the previous move, it would simply represent a temporary halt in the rise. If this happens at previous supply areas, it is expected, and, coupled with smaller volume, would be a safe reaction on which to buy.

In the event it has merely been a bear raid and the reaction is of no more than normal proportions, with a demonstration that the stock or market is unwilling to decline, confidence will be restored and the market may very shortly resume its advance. If repeated profit-taking sales are unable to put much of a dent in the advance, it would indicate that important buying is overcoming whatever profit-taking there is. Also, very often in a bull move, we get sudden reactions late in the day, possibly in the last ten or fifteen minutes. Five or six stocks will weaken, but the general list will not follow it. This would also indicate a healthy market.

Try to plan your strategy outside of regular market hours, preferably after the market closes or before it opens in the morning. Prepare a list of stop-loss-points, breakout-points, all with the idea of avoiding emotional, instantaneous decisions as much as possible. *Never act on impulse!*

Assume that you have made a decision to buy, and the stock is purchased. You are looking for an advance of three or four points, at which point you intend to take profits. But, instead of going up, the stock starts to decline. Now you can either arbitrarily set a limit of two or three points and stop-loss there, or stop-loss below its previous support area, or you can gauge your judgment by the general market. If you have gained the impression that the general market is going to react, then I would not wait for a stop-loss point to be reached, but simply dump the stock "at the market."

Merchants have a saying that the first mark-down is the best one. In the stock market, it is paraphrased to the first loss is the best one.

The important thing to remember in the market is that you must preserve your capital. Anyone can take a profit, but the successful trader is the one who recognizes that he has made a mistake, that he has misjudged the market, and runs like a thief.

In connection with the five or six stocks that you plan on trading actively, you should keep up or purchase some sort of charts—either a bar chart or a point-and-figure chart, or both. If you begin to follow a stock on its chart, you will note certain patterns. Some stocks move in definite arithmetical or geometrical progressions. The stock that has a base of 10 may move to 20, then to 30, then to 40. That is, the important resistance levels will be about ten points apart. Then you will note, perhaps, that after having advanced ten points, the stock may react three or four.

Certain habits of this type cannot be detected until the stock has set up some sort of an advancing or declining pattern. Some stocks may react one-third of their advance; others may react one-half; very volatile issues may even react as much as two-thirds before reversing their trend. But whatever the stock and its habits, you will detect them only if you look for them.

Since most of your time and energy will be utilized in reading the tape, a good way to save time is by subscription to *Technical Stock Reports,* which provides valuable technical data, including a brief analysis based on chart action, of 1000 New York Stock Exchange and American Stock Exchange stocks; *Trendline,* which charts stocks on a daily basis; *Mansfield,* which charts stocks on a weekly basis, and includes a two-year record; and/or Stephens *Graphic Stocks* or *The Stock Picture,* which shows monthly high low records for about twelve years. For a picture of the general market trend, you can subscribe to *Indicator Chart Service,* which provides a graphic presentation of some fifty leading market and business indicators, plus ninety Industry Groups.

By checking the fifteen most active stocks, or the list of new highs or new lows, and then checking these against their chart pictures, you can often catch stocks breaking out into new high ground or new low ground, breaking support or overcoming supply. This can give you some perspective on the stocks in which you trade actively, and also gives you a clue as to the new ones to watch.

The successful trader, of course, keeps a weather eye out for news, both general business and world-wide, of strikes and other labor problems, or anything which might affect the particular stock in which he is trading. In some of the chart services mentioned above, you also get the trend of earnings and dividends. If the stock looks interesting on the tape, you might want to make a quick check on its earnings or dividend trend. You might also keep track of important dividend meeting dates or annual meeting dates and watch out for news about those times. In this way you won't be taken by surprise.

There are some rules of thumb that might prove useful. If a stock opens with a large up gap, it will generally sell half-way back to the gap. That is, it will generally sell half-way back to the point at which it closed on the previous trading day and, if the stock is in a strong uptrend, that would be a good point at which to buy. Or, if a stock is in a downtrend and opens with a large down gap, that point where it recovers half-way to the previous trading day's close would be a good point at which to put out shorts or sell.

The more often a stock approaches a previous supply level or a previous support level before finally breaking through, the stronger the move will be; the longer the stock has been in a trading range, the greater the extent of the move to be expected.

10

UPTICKS, DOWNTICKS, AND TRUE VOLUME

by Don Worden*

As far as I can tell, the term "tape-reading" was probably the original term for what is now generally called "technical analysis." As a matter of fact, the terms are often used interchangeably even today, especially by oldtimers.

Originally, of course, tape-reading referred to the forming of conclusions solely through the use of knowledge abstracted from the ticker tape. Price and/or volume analysis in any form fits into this category. Eventually, perhaps because the summarization of tape data became so involved and far removed from the board room itself, plus the fact that other sources of "non-fundamental" criteria were run upon, technical analysis pretty much replaced tape-reading.

Since then, tape-reading has been relegated by many to its original and more limited meaning, suggesting something that can only be done while actually watching the tape. As an exact definition never

---

*Mr. Worden's DAV's, described in this chapter, are computed for all listed stocks at the Quotron Computer Center. Through an arrangement with Scantlin Electronics, these statistics are disseminated exclusively through Mr. Worden's advisory, statistical, and chart services, published by The Worden Tape Reading Studies, Post Office Box 1776, Des Moines 6, Iowa.

seems to have been determined, I use the term to suit my own methods.

As a tape-reader, the differentiating characteristic of my methods is the fact that I examine individual transactions that have been reported on the tape. Although this area of my work is important, I wish to stress that I do not use such data to the exclusion of other technical tools and methods.

The important elements of conventional technical analysis are price movement and price/volume relationships. Through the study of individual transactions I gain a greater insight into these forces than a conventional technician would. For example, I can often spot unusual volume earlier than would be possible by studying lumped volume, as it appears in the daily newspapers. This is because the unusual incidence of large blocks, especially in the early stages, is often hardly perceptible in the overall picture.

Point and figure charts imply accumulation or distribution, but it is usually necessary to wait for a breakout to determine which is the case. By a build-up of large blocks on either "upticks" or "downticks," it is often possible to anticipate the direction of the breakout to come (not to mention the time of the breakout). Similarly it often prevents being whipsawed, as happens after a false breakout. (If the price movement in a congestion area on a P & F chart suggests accumulation, but I find no ratification by large block activity—I steer clear.)

So, you see, as a tape-reader I not only study volume and price action, but I study these things in terms of the implied sponsorship behind them. This is done by segregating the larger transactions from the smaller ones. The reason for this is the basic premise that big money tends to be smarter money. A secondary premise is that big money movements, right or wrong, have an important causal effect on the direction of a stock's price. If the floating supply of a stock is shortened, it becomes easier for the stock to rise and vice versa.

Where does tape-reading fit in with other technical tools? This is the way I think of it. The most widely used chart is the bar chart. I use it extensively myself, daily basis, weekly basis, and monthly basis.

For a clear picture of price action, unencumbered by the necessity of trying to graph time and volume simultaneously I go to the P & F chart.

Many other investors, I'm sure, are like me. For the ultimate perspective of price movement, they use the P & F chart. But where is the counterpart in volume study?

Through my *Tape Reading Studies* many investors will find the same solution I have. For a pure and revealing picture of volume— nothing is so revealing as a tabulation of large blocks.

Large Block Analysis—How it Works

As large blocks pass on the tape they often cause small imbalances in supply and demand. These larger transactions often take place at a higher price than the immediately preceding transaction or at a lower price than the immediately preceding transaction. The respective terms for these cases are "uptick" and "downtick."

Of course, upticks and downticks occur on all-sized transactions. Any change in price is either an uptick or a downtick.

The relevance of upticks and downticks in large transactions is that they so often, because of their size, are the sole cause of these imbalances. The simple proof for this is that price changes occur with greater frequency on large transactions than on small transactions. They often tip off whether they represent big money moving in or moving out. (At the very least they tip off the ability of the market to absorb such transactions.)

While a stock might appear to be in a stalemated and dull position, persistent and consistent upticks might be taking place, which to the tape-reader represent a constant and vivid rehearsal of what is to happen to the price action eventually on a broader scale as it breaks out on the upside. The same is true in reverse on the downside.

Time and time again we see that tape-reading can tell us that what a stock appears to be doing is only temporary or false. Nothing is more vivid than to watch repeated big money downticks occurring in a stock moving up; or to watch repeated upticks in a stock moving down. It is next to a certain indication of a reversal to come.

On the other hand nothing is more suspicious than observing a stock moving up or down even on large volume without a respectable ratification of the move by big money activity. You see, the essence of what we look for is a contradiction of trend by the direction of big money pressures—whether the trend happens to be up, down, or sideways.

Tape-reading is often referred to as an art because it is inexact. This is true of all technical analysis and, in fact, all stock market analysis. There are exceptions to all characteristic patterns.

The tape-reader is not nearly the slave to trends that another technical analyst virtually must be. He does not need to wait until the price moves decisively upward or decisively downward. The tape-reader is able to anticipate at a much earlier time whether a chart pattern is likely to break out on the upside or on the downside. He is also much more likely to be able to recognize any sort of a false move that a chart formation produces.

While the chartist must rely quite often on rather remotely implied characteristic formations to suggest accumulation or distribution, the tape-reader is often able to detect these phenomena before anything noticeable occurs on a chart at all. He is also in a position to put more confidence in the inferences he draws.

Check It On the Tape

Until recently there were only two possible approaches to the art of tape-reading. One was to sit and watch the tape all day long. This of course, is extremely difficult. The live tape has its advantages, but trying to watch more than one stock at a time is very difficult. And who has time even to sit and watch one stock day after day?

A better approach to tape-reading, in fact the only feasible approach, has been the use of the daily lists of transactions published by Francis Emory Fitch, Inc. Even bringing these transactions into a summarized enough form so that they can be used, however, is a staggering job. Only specialists in tape-reading can really devote much time to it. And at that they have quite a voluminous task to tackle more than a few stocks.

A stock, before a commitment is made, should be studied exhaustively. If you take a standard statistical publication such as *Standard & Poor's Stock Reports* you will be able to find many situations that offer unusual and very subtle—almost hidden—potential. You'll have to study each stock carefully and at length. You would be lucky to find an interesting situation in one of every hundred stocks you studied. The time consumed would be prohibitive.

Tape-reading can give you leads. It is gratifying that so many of the stocks showing unusual activity turn out to be interesting fundamental situations when investigated thoroughly. By confining your exhaustive fundamental investigations to just the stocks that are introduced to you through unusual activity, you might expect to find interesting situations in a third or perhaps even a much higher percentage of the cases you study.

Before you buy a stock, before you sell a stock—check it on the tape. While you hold a stock, from time to time "check it on the tape."

Tape-Reading and Modern Technical Analysis

All technical price and volume data used is summarized tape-reading. The main tools of technical analysis are:

1. Price patterns: resistance levels and trends
2. Price-volume correlations
3. Relative strength

These are the essence of modern technical analysis. Actually they are all just summarized tape-reading. There was a time perhaps when a person's impression of volume and price was merely what he could observe on the tape. Such matters as relative strength (how well a stock is performing compared to other stocks or other groups) were based to a great extent upon the mental agility and memory of a person watching the tape.

It was inevitable that summarizations would occur. Not everybody with ability was a walking adding machine with a photographic memory to boot. And so came charts, probably P & F charts first, but they all came, bar charts, daily basis, weekly basis, and corresponding lumped volume totals.

It appears that there was some reticence in using summarized figures in the early days. Probably a distrust of the accuracy of the figures kept the big operators from wandering too far from the ticker where they could see for themselves. And then—back around the turn of the century there weren't many listed stocks and usually those giving a real interesting play could be counted on your fingers.

But with ever more active stocks, more and better informed traders and investors, charts and their like inevitably became almost necessities. The tape-readers became "technicians."

More and more sophisticated methods were developed until innovations became encompassed which departed from actual tape-reading data (i.e., price and volume data). New techniques were found, such as short interest and odd lot analysis. (It is curious, perhaps, that many more innovations have been developed for the study of the market as a whole than for individual stocks.)

All of this complication in a sense amounts to progress, although to no avail. Technical analysis is a satellite science. It is the competition between investors to be better observers of what the market is actually doing in such a way that inferences can be drawn as to what it will most likely do.

Progress in this science is not basically an improvement. It just makes the game tougher. Craftier bettors do not make faster horses— nor more money go out the pay windows. Nobody can ever invent a system or a method that will make everybody a winner. Only a minority can come out ahead in the long run. More highly developed methods simply make it more difficult to stay out of what I call the "creeping majority."

In any event most progress in technical analysis, whether desirable or not, has been more or less valid and we're stuck with it. Newer methods are more logical, less subjective, and more error-free than plain old tape-reading. Most of the essential elements have been preserved in the summarization. The principles remain the same.

However, one single most important element has been lost in ordinary technical summarization. This, as luck would have it, is the most important of all. It is the analysis of large blocks.

Along with this is lost the most important area of technical analysis—a feel for sponsorship, a feel for whether the buying in a stock is "good buying" or "bad buying." Lost is the basic rationale of the market place: the fact that stocks, like davenports, are bought wholesale and sold retail. That there are never-ending cycles of "accumulation" followed by a "mark up" and finally "distribution." *And that the whole market place, the rumors, the news, the nonsense, the enthusiasm and the post mortems are geared to this basic phenomenon.* Talk it down when you want to buy it—talk it up when you want to sell it.

Many an investor has sniggered at the incorrigible tip-hunter who whispers over the telephone, "Come on, what are 'they' buying? Where are the big boys making their move?" Foolish as this type of bird is, he's asking a question that more people should be asking: "What are the big boys doing?" Corny as it sounds, the big boys are still doing just what they were doing thirty, fifty and seventy-five years ago: buying low and selling high.

True Volume

I have developed a system of determining the technical strength or weakness of a stock which I regard as a whole new dimension, rather than simply another way of indexing or looking at the same old price/volume data. Consequently, I believe it definitely can broaden a technician's perspective by at least 50%. It does not relieve him of the necessity of judgment, experience, and skill—but it can greatly increase the effectiveness of these personal attributes. I tabulate volume at the most basic level in such a way that I come up with a qualitative as well as a quantitative index. I measure (through the use of a trained staff) whether the TRUE VOLUME of a stock is favoring the upside or the downside.

You see, the volume figures that occur in your daily or weekly newspaper are not TRUE VOLUME figures. That is not to say that these newspaper figures are inaccurate or not useful. It is just to say that volume "lumped together" for the day may or may not concur with the TRUE VOLUME story. The TRUE VOLUME story can only be found by analyzing the separate individual transactions as they occur and are reported on the tape.

Before I explain precisely how we are able to derive TRUE VOLUME Indexes, let me show you a startling example of the great difference between the ability of TRUE VOLUME to peg the underlying balance of supply and demand as compared to a conventional volume measurement.

An experienced technician can get a pretty fair impression of conventional volume/price relationships by looking at an ordinary bar chart. If the price goes up most of the time as volume increases, or vice versa, it's not hard to see. However, a number of refinements have been devised to make this relationship easier to see. This is done by tabulating the total volume on price increase days (generally termed buying pressure) and comparing such totals to the amount of volume accrued on price decrease days. Technicians have used such methods for decades. The newest such method is called On Balance Volume. The buying pressure or selling pressure are determined day by day by the method just described. A running cumulative total is kept. On up days the volume is added to the running total. On down days the volume is subtracted.

On Balance Volume represents a good simple way to bring conventional price/volume relationships into a good clear perspective, so I have decided to use it in an example. *Chart 2* is a regular daily basis bar chart of Monsanto. The period covered is from the beginning of September 1963 to the end of December 1963. The On Balance Volume line brings into focus the essence of the relationship between the price plottings and the volume plottings.

When the OBV line goes up it means there is more volume on the upside days. When the OBV line goes down it means there is more volume on the downside days. (The bias might be caused, of course, simply because there are a greater number of either upside or downside days.) Thus On Balance Volume necessarily is pretty well wedded to the trend of the price movement itself. Interpretations must be based on the relative degree of resistance the On Balance Volume Line demonstrates to one or the other direction of the price line.

Chart 2   MONSANTO

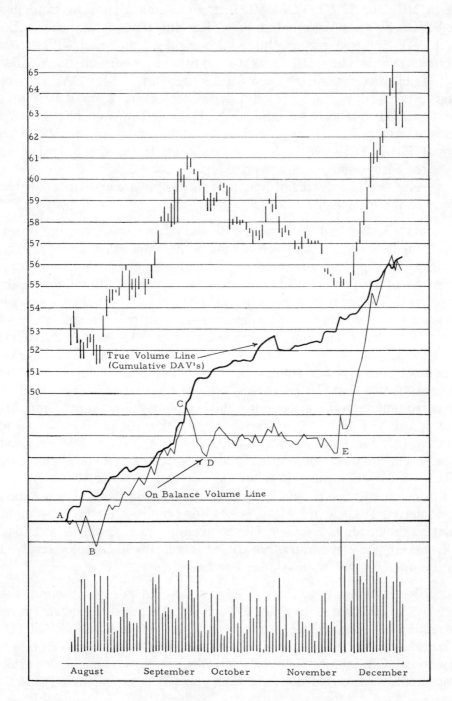

The other line on *Chart 2* is a cumulative tabulation of TRUE VOLUME. The TRUE VOLUME line represents a running total just as the On Balance Volume line does. The difference is that the TRUE VOLUME line is a running total of our daily computed *Differential Activity Values*. These DAV's, as we call them for short, are not wedded to the net price movement even for a single day. A plus DAV may be registered the day of a decline in price or vice versa. A small DAV may be registered on a heavy volume day and a large DAV may be registered on a relatively lighter volume day. In other words the DAV's often reveal TRUE VOLUME to be quite different from what might seem to be the case based on the net price change for a day in relation to the total volume. (The details of how this is possible are explained further along in the monologue.)

Since TRUE VOLUME on a day-to-day basis is often quite different from the conventional volume story, it is not surprising that the pattern developed by a cumulative DAV line might be quite different from the pattern of a cumulative On Balance Volume line. Refer again to *Chart 2*. There are two areas on this chart which reveal the contrast in the ability of these two volume methods to tell the real story of what is ahead, despite actual immediate net price movement. First refer to the space between Point A and Point B on the On Balance Volume line. Both types of volume were tabulated from Point A, starting at zero. Notice that On Balance Volume immediately started logging negative figures and consequently the cumulative line started moving downward. This was in response to the fact that the price was moving downward. (Please observe this carefully on the chart.) In contrast to *both* On Balance Volume and the net price movement notice that TRUE VOLUME immediately sprang upward. Despite the fact that net price changes were giving ground, the cumulative DAV's revealed that internal TRUE VOLUME was totalling higher on upside movement than on downside movement. Hence accumulation could be assumed to be taking place, meaning that the situation was likely to be resolved on the upside—which, of course, it was.

Whereas Point A to Point B covers a minor price correction, the distance from Point C to Point E represents a more important price correction of intermediate proportions. Once again TRUE VOLUME is revealed to be on the upside, while the net price pattern is trending downward. On Balance Volume, responding as it must to the net price movement, also moved down in that Point E is lower than Point C.

However, it should also be pointed out that On Balance Volume showed more resistance to decline than the price itself—best shown by the fact that Point E held just above Point D. The practical use of such resistance is doubtful since such an observation couldn't be made until Point E was a thing of the past and the renewed upswing was well under way. The steady upward movement of the TRUE VOLUME line on the other hand, might have been ample justification for buying into the stock throughout the reaction from Point C to Point E. (We might point out that to comply with SEC requirements we purposely chose an example that has not been among our recommendations. We do have knowledge, however, that some of our subscribers bought heavily into this stock during the reaction from Point C to Point E on the strength of what TRUE VOLUME was revealing.)

I wish to make it clear that my purpose in this comparison has not been to criticize On Balance Volume. Since we make use of conventional volume techniques in conjunction with our own data, I am more or less acknowledging the value of any system which helps put conventional volume into clear perspective. Some of our subscribers are using On Balance Volume method in conjunction with our data and others are so using the Lowry volumatic figures. The more ways you have of looking at something the more meaning you are likely to detect —if for no other reason than that your concentration will be increased by devoting a lot of time to juggling various data around. For this reason I wish to stress that my methods are not designed to conflict with any valid approaches to analyzing stock trends—whether they be technical, fundamental or both.

Different minds and different temperaments run in different channels. If you have progressed to a point where certain techniques seem to agree with your constitution, I suggest you work my TRUE VOLUME data into your present program. I fail to see how it could result in anything but an improvement in your results—very possibly a dramatic improvement. On the other hand, if you just throw away valuable experience by completely disrupting your present methods you might find it necessary to serve a long apprenticeship just to get back where you were.

The development of effective trading skills is a highly personal and evolutionary process. In the long run you have to teach yourself by rediscovering, so to speak, the theories and practical applications that others may try to teach you.

Before going on to a more detailed discussion of how TRUE VOL-
UME data is derived, I would like to clarify one other matter pertaining
to the comparative study brought out on *Chart 2*. We do not ordinarily
make use of cumulative totals. The cumulative DAV line on *Chart 2*
was prepared simply as a means of providing a fair comparison between
TRUE VOLUME and On Balance Volume. On Balance Volume is always prepared according to the cumulative method. We prefer the use
of moving totals for a number of reasons which we shall explain here
later—after you have become better acquainted with the actual method
of computation of the Differential Activity Values.

The Background of True Volume

You have seen a classic example of the penetrative technical insight that TRUE VOLUME makes possible. The system of measurement
does not relieve the investor of the necessity of interpretation. TRUE
VOLUME does not always have a correct answer even for the most
experienced observer. But those of us who appreciate and are even grate-
ful for the difficulties which keep success exclusive are able to see the
great gap between the reliability and usability of this new technical dimension and conventional methods that have been so long in use.

At the very worst TRUE VOLUME measurement will invariably
reveal the same insight as conventional volume observations, such as
On Balance Volume. At best it is incomparable—a tool that the technical connoisseur savors on the one hand, while partaking of its practical
fruits on the other hand.

Having tasted the startling capabilities of TRUE VOLUME you
are asking, how can merely a different method of measurement per-
form so differently from the conventional figures technicians have been
using and heavily relying on for decades? The answer, as I have indicated, lies in the basis of the data. Our staff actually tears volume
down to the smallest pieces. We examine each and every transaction
that passes on the tape. Our methods of computation are not kept se-
cret and I intend demonstrating the technique for you as soon as I have
filled you in on a little more background material.

When I originally began experimenting with individual transactions, my primary interest was to determine whether large transactions
(1000 shares and larger) fell in contrasting patterns to the majority of
transactions which, of course, are most often 100 shares. The rationale

I was trying to prove was simple and logical. If it is true that stock market trading cycles are typical merchandising situations, wherein a more informed element tends to buy low (wholesale accumulation) and sell high (retail distribution) to a less sophisticated element, wouldn't it be probable that the more informed element would tend to trade in larger lots? Wouldn't it also follow that larger lot trading, given impetus by a different type of investor, would tend to fall in patterns contrasting with the pressures revealed by volume as a whole? If you can therefore determine whether large lots seem to be exerting inflow or outflow patterns, either in a stock or in the market, you might conclude that either accumulation or distribution is taking place. The idea is to move in and out with the "big money." Most of my earlier explanatory material examines this theory at length. I might add that while my methods and certain of my attitudes have steadily changed, I still regard this as the most important rationale in technical analysis. All great speculators have realized this since long before my or your time. (Strangely enough, we can never know for sure that the rationale is correct—only that it gives birth to methods that consistently seem to work.)

At first I experimented systematically only with transactions larger than $100,000. To indicate how rare such transactions are you might consider that out of the usual twenty thousand or so transactions that occur in a day's trading on the New York Stock Exchange, there are seldom more than fifty transactions larger than $100,000.

I started tabulating these transactions in 1959. Later my staff ran them retrospectively to the beginning of 1957. The $100,000 Indexes continue to be one of the most important market timing tools used in my advisory service. This is discussed elsewhere. The point I wish to make here is that my $100,000 Indexes did indeed prove, and every day continue to prove, that large transactions do fall into meaningful patterns contrasting with volume as a whole. The two most vital characteristics of large transactions are:

1. They have an ability to contradict over-all price movements by exerting repetitious pressure patterns in the opposite direction.

2. They tend to reverse the direction of their pressures (up or down) ahead of reversals in the price direction.

How do we determine in which direction individual transactions are exerting pressure? This is simple. We use "upticks" and "downticks." If there is no change in price from the immediately preceding transaction, you have neither an "uptick" nor a "downtick" but an "unchanged," which is of little or no use for analytical purposes.

By determining whether the greater amount of activity is occurring on "upticks" or on "downticks" you can determine whether a balance of upward or downward pressures are being exerted. These "upticks" and "downticks" can be manipulated in a variety of ways to form numerical indexes. In the case of $100,000 transactions we use ratios, which are explained in another monologue. (In the case of TRUE VOLUME we use moving totals, which give effect to the volume of activity as well as the direction of the pressures.)

After my $100,000 transaction experiments convinced me that large transactions could reliably be expected to form meaningful pressure patterns, I began to look for a method of indexing transactions for individual stocks. Not that I wasn't utilizing large transactions in my individual stock analysis. It was only that the method I used was quite unsystematic. As a matter of fact I had to overcome a certain mental block that somehow made me suspicious of whether "indexing" individual transactions in individual stocks would constitute some sort of artistic heresy.

In conjunction with conventional volume analysis I used to simply scan transaction lists for large transactions. The idea was to find noticeable or obvious patterns in large transactions that conflicted with conventional volume analysis. Of course, it worked; but it was foolish to rely so heavily upon subjective impressions and human memory. Subtle patterns, of course, more often than not went unnoticed. And the time consumed made it impossible to watch more than just a few stocks at a time. This remained true even after I began publishing "Tape Reading Sheets," which were summarized lists of large individual transactions with notations of whether they had occurred on "upticks" or "downticks." Nevertheless my old "Tape Reading Sheets" were the best tool to be found at the time and they paved the way for my individual stock indexes called *Activity Values,* which eventually resulted in the ultimate unarguable method of measuring TRUE VOLUME: *The Worden Differential Activity Values.*

My original indexes for individual stocks (the old style Activity Values) were inaugurated in January 1963 and were published for a year with excellent results. The exact method of computation was complicated and no longer matters. The definitive characteristic was that they were strictly a "big money" index. They were computed once a week from all transactions of 1000 shares or larger, later from transactions of 500 shares or larger. The indexes took the form of plus or minus numbers expressing the amount and extent of big money pressures affecting any given stock over a week's time. Many of our charts still carry the old style Activity Values up until November 21, 1963.

The success of the old Activity Values in spotting big money buying and selling pressures increased our subscribership greatly and I was able to justify considering the possibilities of more elaborate tabulations which would necessitate enlarging our statistical staff. Effective as the old Activity Values were, I had become aware of certain distortions resulting occasionally because of the method of computation. They also lacked flexibility, especially in that we could not conveniently compute longer term indexes (such as our present 40 day Differential Activity Values.) We were forced to use only weekly figures—no more, no less.

More important—there was one striking error of logic in the old Activity Values. It stems from this: although it can be said that big money activity is more significant than small money activity, there is no logical place to draw the line between what constitutes "big money" activity and what does not. For purposes of tabulating the old Activity Values we had selected an arbitrary point above which constituted "big money." As I mentioned earlier, at first this was 1000 shares, later we dropped to 500 shares and above.

Not that there was anything wrong with the arbitrary cut-off. As far as they went, the old Activity Values measured "big money" activity just as our $100,000 Indexes measure "big money" activity. The question was—did they measure all "big money" activity which, after all, is often expressed quite subtly. Who is to say that an unusual repetition of 200, 300, and 400 share transactions are not just as significant as a couple of 1000 share transactions? It is possible for a trader to accumulate or distribute a lot of stock in a variety of transactions of various sizes. The important question is whether the average size of "downticks" is smaller or larger than the average size of "upticks." It is a simple matter of thinking in relatives—not absolutes. Is the upside attracting more volume or is the downside attracting more volume—relatively speaking?

I knew that indexes that could fully answer these questions would have to be much more sensitive than the Activity Values I was using. They would have to be based on all transactions. But, I asked myself, if I tabulate *all* volume won't I be right back where everybody else is? What about all my work with "big money" activity?

The Logic of True Volume

It was then that I discovered that it was possible to tabulate *all* transactions from 100 shares and up without relinquishing the advantages of a true "big money" index. I found that if I total all volume on "upticks" and all volume on "downticks" they will usually total about the same amount on a given day, whether there is a price increase or a decline. In other words true upside volume and true downside volume are usually pretty much of a washout if you subtract one from the other.

For example, let us assume that on a certain day XYZ Corporation has traded in nothing but 100 share lots. Total volume is 10,000 shares. Net price change has been up half-a-point. Let's assume that twenty of the transactions (2000 shares) were "unchanged." The other eighty transactions (8000 shares) occurred on either "upticks" or "downticks." Let's assume that all ticks were no more nor less than one-eighth-of-a-point. Question: How many more "upticks" were there than "downticks?" Think about it before you go on.

Answer: there would be four more "upticks" than "downticks". There would be one extra uptick for each one-eighth-of-a-point in the net gain (four-eighths). There would be a total upside volume of 4200 shares and a total downside volume of 3800 shares, leaving a differential of 400 shares. Here it is in table form:

Unchanged: 20 at 100 shares	2,000 shares
Upticks: 42 at 100 shares	4,200 shares
Downticks: 38 at 100 shares	3,800 shares
Total volume:	10,000 shares
Differential (Upticks less Downticks):	400 shares

Now let's take the same example and multiply the total volume by four making 40,000 shares. Everything stays proportionately the same. The net increase is still four-eighths of a point. What is the new differential between upside and downside volume? The answer is more important than the last one. The answer is that the differential remains the same—400 shares. There would be 8000 shares "unchanged." 16,200 shares on "upticks" and 15,800 shares on "downticks," leaving a meager differential of 400 shares upside volume, despite the fact that the stock advanced half-a-point on what would be described as heavy volume (40,000 shares). This is what I mean when I say that small transactions tend to wash each other out if they are characterized by small transactions. Here it is in a table again:

Unchanged: 80 at 100 shares .... 8,000 shares
Upticks: 162 at 100 shares .... 16,200 shares
Downticks: 158 at 100 shares .... 15,800 shares

Total volume: 40,000 shares
Differential (Upticks less Downticks):   400 shares

Now let's carry this example a little further to show you just what I'm driving at. Total volume is still 40,000 shares and everything is almost the same. Net gain: five-eighths of a point. Another little exception: there are not 400 separate 100 share transactions making up the 40,000 shares. There is one 10,000 share transaction on a "downtick." 8000 shares are "unchanged," leaving 220 transactions of 100 shares each that occurred on either "upticks" or "downticks." We know there must be five more "upticks" than "downticks" because there are five-eighths of a point net gain. There must be 113 "upticks" and 108 "downticks" (including the one 10,000 share transaction that occurred on a "downtick"). The question is—was there an upside or a downside volume differential and what did it amount to in shares?

Answer: There were 113 "upticks" at 100 shares each, making a total upside volume of 11,300 shares. There were 108 "downticks," 107 at 100 shares each and one at 10,000 shares making a downside total of 20,700 shares. This makes a downside differential of 9400 shares—a very large downside differential indeed, and on a day that otherwise might be described as a good advance on heavy volume. In actuality TRUE VOLUME heavily favored the downside. Although there were more "upticks" than "downticks," the average size "downtick" was larger—thus causing a downside differential. Here is the table to make it clearer:

Unchanged: 80 at 100 shares .... 8,000 shares
Upticks: 113 at 100 shares .... 11,300 shares
Downticks at 100 shares (107)................ 10,700 shares
Downticks at 10,000 shares (1) .... 10,000 shares
Total downtick volume .... 20,700 shares

Total volume: 40,000 shares
Differential (Downticks less Upticks): 9,400 shares

You can see by this example that significant TRUE VOLUME is really controlled and can only be controlled by large transactions. Volume may be great or small, but the differential between upside and downside TRUE VOLUME will remain minimal without the effects of large transactions. TRUE VOLUME then is really a total volume measurement which automatically gives effect to "big money activity pressures."

The implications of this are much more widely significant than you might think. It shows that volume measured in its ultimate form is meaningless unless "big money" activity lends a bias to either the upside or the downside. All volume measurement then, in any form, is really a method for discernment of the effects of "big money" activity. Most conventional methods are quite crude, of course, especially when you consider that they are trying to measure precisely the same thing we are but have to rely on only one price change per day together with one volume figure.

In the Monsanto example (p. 69) On Balance Volume was able to show relative resistance during a declining phase. To this extent the effects of "big money" activity were able to show through the lumping of daily totals. But On Balance Volume was unable to keep from posting a negative total while the net price gave ground. It was only through detailed tabulations of individual transactions that we were able to show TRUE VOLUME as it actually gave effect to "big money" activity. TRUE VOLUME showed the balance to be on the upside, even while the stock was declining.

For all practical purposes you have been learning how we tabulate and compute our Differential Activity Values. These are our new and ultimate TRUE VOLUME measurements. They were introduced into our service in November 1963. Total "uptick" volume and total "downtick" volume are tabulated. Then the smaller is subtracted from the larger to determine the "differential," which is plus if upside volume is greater and minus if downside volume is greater. The actual figure used in the index has two zeros rounded off. Thus in the first two examples above we had an upside "differential" of 400 shares. This would be expressed as DAV +4, a small and insignificant figure. In the last example we had a downside "differential" of 9400 shares. Round off two zeros and you have DAV −94, a figure more than large enough to be significant. There are two modifications used in deriving the figure, however, which we shall bring out shortly.

Now let's take an actual example of a day's trading. There are often hundreds of transactions in a day's trading for a given stock, but for the sake of simplicity we have chosen a less active example. Remember, it is not the number of transactions or the amount of total volume which gives the most signicant effect to the TRUE VOLUME differential. It is the average size of the transactions which is the weightiest determinant.

This example appeared in one of our weekly reports. It is a day of trading in Loew's Theatres—the day, November 22, 1963, a day of tragedy. The transactions are arranged in the order that they occurred:

1. 300 16⅞ uptick		7.	100 16¾ no change
2. 300 17 uptick		8.	100 16¾ no change
3. 500 16⅞ downtick		9.	100 16¾ no change
4. 300 16⅞ no change		10.	100 16¾ no change
5. 700 17 uptick		11.	10,000 16⅞ uptick
6. 100 16¾ downtick		12.	100 16¾ downtick

Notice that we have designated for you whether each transaction is an "unchanged," "uptick," or a "downtick." Actually you should be able to see this for yourself by relating the price of each transaction to that of the preceding transaction. The exception is the "opening" or first transaction of the day. This must be related to the last transaction of the preceding day, which we have not shown. Here is how it totals:

Unchanged .... 700 shares
Upticks .... 11,300 shares
Downticks .... 700 shares
Total Volume .... 12,700 shares
Differential in shares .... 10,600 shares
Differential (Index form): .... +106

This in essence is the way Differential Activity Values, our TRUE VOLUME indexes, are derived each day for each stock. There are two modifications:

1. All transactions of 100 shares are omitted. It was found that 100 share transactions always wash each other out almost in entirety. Since trades of 100 shares are the smallest possible transactions to appear on the tape, they are reduced to zero reference for purposes of determining differentials between upside and downside volume. The inclusion of 100 share transactions never affects the final Differential Activity Value significantly (usually only one or two DAV points).

2. The opening transaction is exempt. This is because "openings" generally represent an accumulation of overnight orders. They do not show the effects of "free trading," which we are trying to capture. Experimentation has shown us that they interfere with the ability of TRUE VOLUME to contradict net price movements, because "openings" are usually moving in the same directions as the over-all price. (We also omit mid-day openings that result from trading in a stock being closed down, for some reason or another, and then reopened.)

Here then is the trading in Loew's Theatres on November 22 with asterisks indicating the eligible transactions. The DAV turns out +105, rather than +106 as in the unmodified example.

1.	300 16⅞ opening	7.	100 16¾ no change
*2.	300 17 uptick	8.	100 16¾ no change
*3.	500 16⅞ downtick	9.	100 16¾ no change
4.	300 16⅞ no change	10.	100 16¾ no change
*5.	700 17 uptick	*11.	10,000 16⅞ uptick
6.	100 16¾ downtick	12.	100 16¾ downtick

Here is a table of the tabulation of Loew's Differential Activity Value for the day, November 22, 1963:

Upticks	11,000 shares
Downticks	500 shares
Differential in shares	10,500 shares
Differential Activity Value:	+105

The closing price of 16¾ in Loew's that day was unchanged from the preceding day's closing price. In fact, you will notice that the closing price for the day was one-eighth below the opening price. Without individual transaction analysis you might have concluded that the stock was churning or giving ground on increasing volume. The TRUE VOLUME story, however, is revealed only in our unique index (DAV +105). It is not surprising that the stock rallied for several weeks following this occurrence. It is also interesting to note that the 10,000 share uptick was the second last transaction of the day. We don't know precisely at what time it occurred, but we know that the last nine transactions occurred after 1:00 P.M. So the news that President Kennedy had been shot was definitely out before the 10,000 share transaction occurred. This is a very obvious case of disturbing news being used as a smoke screen for a large purchase.

Flying By the Seat of Your Pants

I once read in an old out-of-print book that a good tape-reader acts without thinking. He follows his first impressions. An unknown previous owner of the book had written in the margin next to this contention: "Important!"

I smiled and thought about it for a while, because it was an appealing thought. It was also, I thought, a dangerous oversimplification.

I suppose any skilled subjective technique works best by way of the subconscious mind. A "hunch," so to speak, is an *educated* guess. When engaged in tape-reading, a person could not stop to think about everything he has ever learned about the subject. He must act with reasonable promptness and decisiveness, which means relying heavily upon intuition.

However, intuition is not magic. It is really only the subconscious forming of conclusions. Any conclusion is subject to error. Your subconscious mind is as much the slave to experience as is your conscious mind.

For example, a professional baseball player reacts automatically, which is to say without applying full conscious thought to his every movement. But could you expect to knock a ball over a major league fence just because you were relaxed and acting upon impulse? Of course not. First you need ability and experience. As a baseball player acquires these requisites, nobody needs to tell him not to think too much. He won't have time to think too much.

It is not completely dissimilar with tape-reading. Reliance upon intuition is a practical necessity. It is not, however, the key to effective results. Self-training is the key.

But it is a useful concept and, although that old tape-reader didn't explain it, I think that he was really getting at this. There are no set rules to tape-reading. Effective conclusions are often too complex for ready dissection. Too many factors enter into them. Sometimes you can find a situation that just doesn't ring true—and if you are an experienced tape-reader, you might best take heed of that ringing noise.

The essence of tape-reading is being able to interpret various activities on the tape in light of many, many other factors. It is your *total knowledge* of the stock, the market, the economy, human nature and who-knows-what-else that provides the background for you to decide that what you see on the tape is either bullish or bearish. The same tape action under one set of conditions might yield an opposite conclusion to one under another set of conditions.

For example, after John Glenn made his historical space flight he reported that he had been able to see rivers over the United States. He reported, however, that he wouldn't have known they were rivers merely from how they appeared, which was as gray lines upon the earth. He stated that he was familiar with the territory in which he spotted them and by observing the relationship of larger formations such as mountains or bays, he was able to infer what the gray lines were. In other words, it was out of his total knowledge that he was able to recognize what otherwise might have remained mysterious gray lines. It is out of our total knowledge that we are sometimes able to recognize individual transactions for what they really are.

I have not infrequently had this sort of experience. After reading the tape on a stock and coming to a conclusion, I have gone back some time later to recheck or organize my original conclusions more closely. I have often found the tape action the second time to be cold and uncommunicative. The tape seemed ambiguous. The first time through my impressions seemed much more clear-cut.

I believe this to be partly a matter of concentration and partly a matter of something else. In going through the second time, it is like seeing an old movie on TV. If you've seen it before, you know the ending and the original suspense is not there. In other words, your concentration is not held tightly in the fascination of expectancy.

The second cause is that the many, many other little corroboratory bits of knowledge nibbling at my reasoning centers were no longer nibbling. A feeling for the state of the market, a reaction to a bit of news—these things cannot be recreated. The next time they're just not there, or at least not to the same degree. The lesson, of course, is that the transactions alone do not produce meanings. Vivid insights result from comparisons with other facts, the more immediate and alive the better.

We Are Eavesdroppers

Enough of flavor. Let's back up a bit. We know now that a tape-reader studies individual transactions—most especially large ones.

Why? Before you ever look for a large transaction, let's get a concrete idea of why we should want to do so in the first place.

The basic answer is simple. We are eavesdroppers. We are not insiders. We know better than to trust tips. So we try a little spying in hopes of hearing what the insiders are saying—not with their mouths, but with their money.

If we knew enough, perhaps we would have no use for tape-reading. It is a method of filling in an inevitable void—the unknown. To a great extent a tape-reader tries to emulate somebody who knows something more than the tape-reader himself does.

Good tape-reading should stop short of emulation, however. A large transaction makes a better clue than it does a crutch. Our primary purpose is simply to detect "big money" activity. The working assumption is that big money is synonymous with informed money. If we observe what appears to be informed money activity in a stock, it gives us a basis for further exploration. Something is brewing. We try to find out what and why. Chances are at least a part of those answers will have to come from sources other than the stock tape.

Of course, we also hope to detect whether informed sources are accumulating or distributing a stock. If we can find adequate corroboratory evidence that they are doing the right thing, we are likely to follow them. To this extent we are imitators.

We might use tape action as a means of uncovering interesting stocks. We might use the tape only for a clue to better timing. No matter what use we put it to, tape-reading is basically an artificial or satellite form of analysis. This is true of all technical analysis. I believe that most "technicians" would do well to remember this.

Tape-Reading and Technical Analysis

Just where does tape-reading fit in with other forms of technical analysis? In my opinion all technical analysis (almost all) is boiled-down tape-reading. Anything that involves the study of price action or the study of volume is a simplified form of tape-reading. Charts, for example, basically represent tape-reading techniques.

Most forms of technical analysis unfortunately have become "oversimplified" tape-reading. This is more in the application than in the tools themselves.

Many if not a majority of "technicians" have come to advocate a complete exclusion of fundamental analysis. This is pure nonsense and it is responsible for the notion in some circles that technical analysis is akin to witchcraft.

The whole idea that there is a "school of technical analysis" and a separate "school of fundamental analysis" is absurd. "Technical analysis" used to be called "tape-reading." Perhaps if it had been left that way all this muddle wouldn't have gotten started. The term "tape-reading" at least doesn't seem to imply an opposition to fundamental facts. Any fundamentalist knows that he must read the tape or some other printed price quotation to find the price of a stock. This in and of itself is technical analysis—simply looking up the price of a stock.

Technical analysis and fundamental analysis are not only inseparable, they are the same thing. Technical analysis is simply the study of the mechanics of how stock prices adjust (or maladjust) to fundamental facts.

If a fundamentalist concludes that the price of a stock should go up, how does he think it is going to get there? In a helium balloon? It is going to go up because supply and demand will cause price responses to fundamental changes. So any fundamentalist who has ever looked up the prices of his stocks in the newspapers is also a technician. So much for that.

The Character of Supply and Demand

Ordinary technical analysis or the study of supply and demand alone implies something like this: the attempt to determine whether the present demand or the future demand or the potential demand is greater than the present, future or potential supply. This sort of quest is based on an assumption that is virtually never questioned. That is, that if demand is greater than supply, prices will rise; and if supply is greater than demand, prices will fall.

Tape-reading has led me to believe that it is not nearly so simple. It is possible for the demand to be greater than the supply while the price is moving down. It is also possible for the supply to be greater than the demand while the price is moving up. Neither supply nor demand affects the market until they are exercised. The most relevant demand at any given moment may be dormant and the same may be said about supply. It depends upon the shrewdness of the buyers and sellers in choosing the correct time to buy. It is for them to decide *when* they play their hands.

This is why the *character* of supply and demand is much more important than a simple quantitative appraisal. Put simply, we could say this: it is not as important to know *what* the demand is at any given time as it is to know *who* is creating the demand. (Most important, of course, is the question of *why* demand exists.)

For tape-readers the *who* is answered by the size of the block. Big blocks are generally assumed to mean big money sources. The *why* is answered by whatever fundamental knowledge we can put together. Often a fundamental insight (a bit of business knowledge) can give more meaning to an otherwise unexplainable technical occurrence; just as technical activity can give meaning to an otherwise unexplainable business fact.

Buying and Selling—Good or Bad?

Most technical analysis is limited to judging supply and demand, past and present. The only clues to the future are based upon inertia, which is to say the assumption that "a trend once begun, continues until it is interrupted." This simply means that if demand at the present is greater than supply, it is a logical assumption that it will not change overnight.

Tape-reading, however, seeks to evaluate the formidability of either supply or demand at the moment, regardless of which is larger. In other words, in a falling market, supply is at least temporarily exceeding demand. But if the sources of demand seem more formidable than the sources of supply, we have the suggestion that the buyers are more right than the sellers. Perhaps the buyers know something that will in time convert the sellers into buyers.

Here, then, we have one of the most fascinating dilemmas in technical analysis. That is, that the study of supply and demand nowhere offers a solution to the constant threat of either "bad buying" or "bad selling." This is the major flaw in technical analysis. Grassroots tape-reading offers the only technical solution to the problem.

More About Bad Buying or Bad Selling

Fundamentals are the basic reason behind ultimate stock moves. Imbalances in supply and demand often occur in direct contradiction to actualities. This causes a stock to move in the incorrect direction. However, such imbalances are only temporary.

A good example of bad selling occurred a few years ago in Chrysler. An extensive amount of accumulation took place on good fundamental grounds in the low 40's. This took many months. In August of 1961 the stock finally broke out on the upside and moved up to the middle 50's quite rapidly. There it stayed for some time until it finally started back down. It didn't take long for it to get down into the high 40's. This downmove, which took place on heavy volume, was in response to an announcement that Chrysler's percentage of industry sales was disappointing. This was an excellent example of poor selling, and it was detectable on both fundamental and technical (tape-reading) grounds.

In the matter of tape-reading it was quite simple. To sum it up, the extended period of accumulation took place on large blocks and the upmove itself took place on large blocks. The downmove, however, was characterized by small transactions. This, even though the over-all volume was heavy.

From a fundamental standpoint the downmove was also quite suspicious. It was not the kind of announcement that falls into the category of an unforeseen event. Chrysler's position, in terms of industry sales, had for years been shaky. The fact that it turned out disappointingly must have at least been anticipated as a distinct possibility on the part of many of the professionals and insiders accumulating at an earlier time. They must, therefore, have accumulated the stock based on some other fundamental reason.

A little investigation, no more than a little, revealed the reason to us. Although the percentage of the industry's sales had dropped, Chrysler had so trimmed its efficiency that it needed only a modest percentage of industry sales to make a substantial profit compared to the year before. So once again on logical fundamental grounds the selling looked quite uninformed. That is the way it turned out. In short order Chrysler rose from the middle 40's to above 60.

An example of bad buying occurred early in 1962. The stock was MGM. For some reason or another a lot of advisory services had recommended the stock. There were also some rather noisy news releases about a European record contract. The stock moved up quite rapidly. It was being so heavily recommended that we examined several months of tape action very carefully. We could find no evidences of big money accumulation preceding the move. Furthermore, the move itself revealed no corroboration by "big money" activity. *The total volume was high and it probably looked very bullish to bar chartists.* To a tape-reader it was a hands-off proposition and, of course, that's the way it turned out.

The Major Difficulty In Tape-Reading

Every stock is different. Every stock has its own personality.

Stirling Moss, once the world's best race driver, says that the greatest difficulty in a race over the same course is that it is constantly changing. You might go around the same curve one hundred times and every time it is a different situation. The texture of the track varies, the weight of your fuel supply, firmness of shock absorbers. These variances demand constant judgment.

Although there is a tendency for high-priced stocks and, of course, highly capitalized stocks to trade in larger quantities, there is no set rule. Aluminium Limited, for the several years I have observed it, never ceases to amaze me in the quantities it trades in—constant large blocks. month after month. The trouble is that they all seem to tell nothing.

In 1959 I watched so many "downticks" in the stock that I wouldn't have been surprised to see it go to zero. The relative performance that followed was not bad at all.

In some stocks, just a lot of 1000 share blocks can tell you somebody is buying all that's available. In others, such blocks are too common to even consider.

A tape-reader must be able to accept the discomfort of never knowing for sure. But this is life. Most people don't have to admit it to themselves. But a tape-reader must. If you can't live with doubt, constantly jockeying with probabilities, you can't be a tape-reader. You would become a mental wreck.

Recently in watching Allied Chemical, if I hadn't really been careful I might have made a needless error. There were several spurts on strong "upticks" of blocks worth $50,000 to $100,000. If I hadn't done a complete analysis I wouldn't have seen the many blocks over $1 million on "downticks" when the stock was actually moving up.

A highly capitalized stock such as this is the only kind of stock a really big trader can operate in for snap profits. There are several stocks in which you can generally observe them come in and out, for what are only fairly limited short term gains. Chrysler is probably one of the best examples of this kind of stock.

What Makes a Good Trading Stock?

Generally speaking most tape-readers would regard the main prerequisite of a good trading stock to be a reasonably large capitalization and well sustained activity.

Such a stock would tend to move rather gradually with only an eighth-of-a-point or so between price changes even on rather large blocks.

There is a good deal to be said about such situations, especially from the standpoint of ease of getting in and out, which in effect is also a safety factor. For short-term trading this is the best type of stock.

At the other extreme is the small capitalized stock which I myself prefer. It does not lend itself, of course, to quick trading, especially if it is low-priced. In practice, a low price on this kind of stock seems to be the rule rather than the exception. There are two advantages in this kind of a stock to the tape-reader.

1. Unusual activity is easier to detect (or at least is easy to detect in an ample enough number of them to provide more trading opportunities than you would ever need). The activity is easier to evaluate and is less often ambiguous.

2. Such stocks are thin issues and a reasonable amount of accumulation makes them even thinner. They are, therefore, fast movers and allow for high percentage gains.

The big disadvantage to these stocks is that if you are trading in large quantities you might have a very difficult time even in small quantities. The price moves are quite wide and it is necessary from a practical standpoint to take comparatively large risks, if they go against you. You can't cut your losses very short without accruing too many of them. Less than 30 percent downside latitudes are usually unwieldy. Also, if they are low-priced the commissions are quite high.

Unforeseen Events

The ultimate question as a tape-reader is not—was an "uptick" a buy or was it a sell, or do a series of "upticks" indicate accumulation or do a series of "downticks" indicate distribution? The ultimate question about any stock is, "Is it to go up or down?"

It does not necessarily follow that a price advance is the inevitable aftermath of accumulation or vice versa about distribution. Smart money and insiders can be wrong, or they can have personal reasons for their actions. The fact remains that unforeseen events do occur, although it is amazing how seldom they do.

This, for example, is what recently happened to Ling-Temco-Vought. There were noticeable indications of informed accumulation while the stock was running up. The litigation which messed everything up must be considered an unforeseen event.

The Billy Sol Estes case is an excellent example of the inescapable danger of the unexpected and of the way pros flee from uncertainty. Commercial Solvents, a strong-looking stock if there ever was one, took a sickening tumble. The company was Billy Sol's major supplier. There is no reason to assume that Commercial Solvents was involved in any of the shady goings-on—but what experienced investor wants to take a chance?

What is the Probability of an "Uptick" Being a "Sell"

The probability of a large block being a "sell" increases in proportion to the chances of being able to make an easy sale in a stock—regardless of whether the block happened to be an "uptick" or a "downtick." The chances of a large block being a "buy" increases proportionately to how much of a buyers' market it seems to be for the stock.

In other words, if a stock is hard to buy the chances of the "upticks" being buys are greater than if the stock is easy to buy.

In actual practice, then, the probability of your ticks being the opposite of what they appear to be varies under many sets of conditions. It depends on what you know about a particular stock and what you can paste together about it.

For example, if a stock has been in a decline, *a long decline*, and has shown signs of bottoming out, and if the stock is extremely unpopular, you have good grounds for being suspicious of the meanings behind "downticks," for this simple reason: due to the unpopularity of the stock it is possible for orders for large amounts to be placed at specific levels. Under these conditions there is always the chance that the price will move down repeatedly and fairly easily to these levels where accumulation takes place. The buy transactions under these conditions could frequently occur on "downticks."

In addition to this, the fact that the stock has come down so far diminishes the probabilities of distribution. "Big money" after all tends to be smart money. Distribution, normally, can be expected to occur at reasonably advanced levels.

What is an Insider?

In actual practice a tape-reader does not rely without question upon the basic premise that big money is smart money. This undoubtedly has elements of relative truth. This I believe, of course, or I wouldn't be a tape-reader in the first place. But insiders can be wrong.

If you don't like the uncertainty of tape-reading, let me warn you about something. The stock market is an uncertainty. A person who faces this, operates with what he can infer through hard work and experience, and learns to make probabilities, *not certainties*, work in his favor—this person will do all right.

He is almost certain to do better than the guy on a never-ending quest for a guarantee. He is absolutely certain to do better than the man who believes he has found a certainty—because that man has caught himself in a trap.

What are insiders? They are first of all officers and important stockholders in companies. But there is another larger group of professional investors: account managers, holders of large estates, independent traders, etc.

The activity of this second group is completely inaccessible except through tape-reading. The first group reports its transactions to the SEC. This is slow knowledge, but accurate—and for that group generally—that's enough. After all, they are not traders.

We regard the first group of insiders as relatively unsophisticated, investment-wise. Remember, they are not professional investors.

Just as sophistication in the world means "world-wise" outside of book-learning—in the stock market it means "market-wise"—outside of business ability.

Remember, people have extremely personal or special reasons for investing in their own companies.

They often, as a matter of fact, do extremely well in growth stocks, because they just hold them through thick and thin. How many investors held Texas Instruments through that entire precipitous climb? I had one friend who bought it at 10, sold it at 20. He had doubled his money! Later he bought it at 100—sold it at 125. He had made 25 points!

The insider in a successful growth stock often naively turns out to be the most sophisticated investor of all. He holds it long. He lets his profits run, as the sophisticated investor should but often mistakenly doesn't. And the outsider often might have as good a grasp of a corporation's business outlook as the insider. But the outsider is in a different frame of mind. He bought the stock to sell and he is trigger-happy. He is attuned to signs of weakness in the price action.

The insider, on the other hand, doesn't buy it to sell. He blissfully doesn't notice the day-to-day fluctuations. He isn't rattled by either strength or weakness, because he bought it to hold.

However, he is holding it for the wrong reason—the reason being that he happens to work there. When I say the wrong reason I mean the wrong reason from a stock market investor's viewpoint. His reasons might be fine. But from the market investor's viewpoint, it is only a coincidence.

The insider *in an enormously successful stock* is generally led by circumstances into making the most sophisticated decisions. After holding through thick and thin, he winds up selling at the right time.

Eventually he notices he is a rich man. This makes him a different man with a different viewpoint. His job for one thing isn't as important to him. He also notices that it was his stock that made him rich. So his attention becomes increasingly concerned with that stock.

He's a smart man. He knows his own business. He can see the rate of growth will slow down soon. He can also see the price of the stock is astronomical compared to earnings and plain common sense tells him it won't last forever. So he sells some of it at just the right time.

You say, "Well, this naive market-wise insider didn't do so badly. Everybody should mimic these naive insiders."

Here, in my opinion, is the rub. There are thousands of insiders who could have had this same experience compared to the relatively few who have actually had it. Think of the many who held their stocks, too, through thick and thin and where did they go? No place! The successful ones were in the right companies. This for all practical purposes is coincidental even though the particular insiders might have contributed greatly to the success.

The investor must decide which is the right company. He must choose from many and then wonder all the way. Of course, he will make more mistakes than the one lucky insider sitting in the right spot. But he will make less than the unlucky insider—sitting in the wrong spot.

So, the insiders we are most interested in mimicking are not necessarily even connected to a company. They are *professional* market-wise investors.

They don't report to the SEC. They might well know more about the probable course of the price action in a stock than the president himself—the president of the company, that is.

As far as I know, tape-reading gives us our only insight into the activities of this group.

Don't Look Too Hard

The more I look at the stock market the more I become convinced of the danger of over-concluding. It is not good to base decisions on fine points—whether these decisions pertain to a chart pattern, tape-reading observations, or fundamental grounds.

It is fine to understand something in the greatest detail. I am not advocating laziness.

However, if you over-intellectualize on anything you are endangering yourself to the possibility of confusing conjecture—even the most informed, sophisticated, and highly polished conjecture—with something that is a real possibility.

Tell-tale signs, real tell-tale signs, are often very difficult to find. They are hidden. But once you find them, they are or should be obvious. It should not take a great amount of conjecture about this-and-that to come to a conclusion. There should be a limited number of premises and a limited number of syllogisms from which to form your conclusion. The more thought steps you have to take, the greater the danger of an erroneous conclusion based upon just one little erroneous step along the way that made all subsequent steps, no matter how skillfully they were taken—erroneous, useless and misleading.

New Plumber In Town

In line with my ideas about things not being too complicated, nor too difficult, if you intend to base conclusions on them, it is my opinion that the hard work comes in learning what to look for in the first place. After you have learned what you are looking for, the task of recognizing something when you see it should be easy. If it's not easy it is not a valid thing upon which to base a conclusion.

It's something like this. A man had a difficult plumbing problem which plumber after plumber failed to solve. One plumber took the entire apparatus apart and put it back and it still worked the same way. He, of course, didn't charge the man.

Finally a new plumber came to town. The man engaged him. He took a look at the situation, pulled a small part out of his tool kit and promptly made a replacement. The whole operation took approximately five minutes. He then sent the man a bill for a hundred dollars. The man said this was plainly absurd for such a small amount of work and for a cheap little repair part. He took the plumber to court.

The judge asked the plumber how much the part had cost and the answer was fifteen cents. He asked him how much of his time he had devoted to the job and he said about five dollars' worth.

"How then do you account for this hundred dollar charge?" asked the judge.

"Fifteen cents for the part, five dollars for the labor, and a mere ninety-four dollars and eighty-four cents for the twenty years it took me to learn how to do it," said the plumber.

Do Insiders Try to Hide Their Movements?

Of course insiders try to hide their movements. But how can they? This is the least of their problems. The big problem is how to buy in a large quantity within a good price range. There will seldom be only one big money investor bent on the same task. So when there is stock for sale, that insider had better buy it—while the buying is good. After he's in it, why should he care who knows it?

How Many Stocks Do You Need?

The trick in tape-reading or, in fact, in stock market analysis in general is not to correctly peg every stock you investigate. The trick is to recognize those few you can peg and those you can't peg. A stock that doesn't reveal enough of itself should be treated the same as a stock that looks downright risky. If you can't be sure—don't play. Wait for the ace.

11

CHARTING WITH SUMMARY DATA

The third main approach to using tape data is through summary figures—high, low, close, and volume. It often proves useful to chart this data. The objective is to find advance signals of *turns* or reversals of existing trends. The *averages* can be useful in determining the general pattern of the market. *Charts* are handy summaries of recent action in individual stocks. Each of these is discussed in this section.

Turn Signals

A turn may be nothing more than a minor move. It may be a rally in a bear market or a dip in a bull market, or it may be the beginning of a change in the major trend.

While turns are important, it must be remembered that major trends do not change without warning. Even though a sharp turn up or down may be the advance signal of an important change of trend, nevertheless there will be ample opportunity for the operator to change his position before a major trend is well under way.

Sharp turns, according to their intensity and the condition of the market, may be due to short covering, frightened selling, false moves, or a forced condition. Sound investors and professional operators take their positions quietly in the dull period which precedes the turn. They have read the handwriting on the wall while the public slept. They *knew* when stocks were a buy or a sale and acted accordingly. It is the unwary public which causes sharp turns by rushing in to cover shorts or distribute stocks. When the public's excitement is over, the market will settle back more nearly to normal. The change of a major trend may be under way, but it will actually start from a more normal base.

If you feel you are bucking the trend take your loss and get out; but unless you do it immediately *wait until the first excitement is over.* Otherwise, you will buy at top and sell at bottom.

Major Turns

Actual major turns in a market generally start from a selling climax; but they have laid their base long before. Before a major turn there is always a long period of accumulation or distribution. This is done under cover of false market moves which cause a period of irregularity. Stocks move erratically, without definite trend.

In the case of an expected downturn (after a long bull market), they go spasmodically higher, hesitate, drop, move upward again, fail to make new highs, describe wide arcs. All this happens before climax selling comes in. It is the signal to the professional operator to get out of the market. The unsuspecting public considers it the signal to buy more stock.

In a bear market before climax selling begins, there is also a period of irregularity. Stocks sell lower, the pivotal issues make new lows, come back, sink again, and then stabilize. The market rallies slightly; then other important stocks sell off and make new lows. Finally the time comes when the *extreme* lows are tested out.

These are the signals of a major turn:

After a long bear market. When the market fails in a sharp test to go below the record lows of that major trend, encountering buying support just above that point, and when both the rail and industrial averages (see below) meet that test at the same time, confirming each other's position, it is an excellent indication that the bear market is over.

No test is infallible, for at any time fundamental conditions may come in which will alter the entire situation. Bear in mind, however, that the important investment interests—whose buying or selling are the underlying factors which determine major trends—are fully conversant with fundamental conditions and discount them in their market activity.

After a long bull market. When the market fails, after repeated efforts, to carry its pivotal issues to new highs, bringing out blocks of stock for sale on every rally upward, and when both rail and industrial averages confirm each other by refusing to make new highs, it is an excellent indication that the bull market is finished. Wise investors have sold before this point. It is the final signal for a downturn.

Minor Turns

When a few stocks run up rapidly, slow down and make another start, and there is high volume at the peak, it means distribution. Watch the general market. If the advance does not proceed across a broad front, lower prices are due.

When popular speculative stocks run up rapidly but the general market does not follow, a crest is near. Get out.

Distress Signals

Distress selling comes into the market because of overburdened margin accounts, forced liquidation from investment accounts, or the fact that some financial house is in trouble. Naturally, distress selling occurs only in bear markets, usually after a long downward trend. It is evidenced by the appearance of large blocks of stock, often thrown on the market for what they will bring. This means a wide margin of prices between sales. When there is any uncertainty, have your broker get you a "floor quote" on the stock. If a large block comes out immediately or soon after "at the bid," you can assume it is forced selling.

Marginal distress selling usually comes into the market between 12:00 and 1:00 or between 2:00 and 3:00.

Forced selling in any market is a danger signal. Do not ignore it. When forced selling is accompanied by increased volume, put your house in order.

Selling Drives

Friday afternoon shortly before close is the favorite time for a selling drive, as stocks need not be delivered until Monday. When the market is moving along uncertain lines and the trend is down, watch for a bear drive Friday afternoon.

Frequently, certain stocks are heavily sold by professional operators to depress the market as a screen for short-covering in the general list. When this is done to mask buying or selling, stocks which can be moved easily are chosen. These are not the usual market leaders because the market leaders have a consistent rate of supply and demand which makes it difficult to move them erratically.

Rail and Industrial Averages*

In following the technical condition of the market, the action of the averages of selected railroad and industrial stocks is an important indicator of what is happening. Even though no other charts are kept, every market operator should have access to reliable charts of these averages and to certain graphs.

Charts of the averages are also valuable for measuring the extent of reactions and for determining support and resistance points. Reactions or rallies normally extend from one-third to one-half of the major movement. Where they pass the halfway point, it is an indication of a reversal of the trend. Secondary reactions or rallies should be in about the same proportion as those of a major move. When they penetrate the lows or highs of the primary movement, a major continuation of the move is indicated.

A change of trend is indicated when, *after a sharp advance or decline, the Rail and Industrial Averages confirm each other* by registering new highs or lows at about the same time. This is a basic chart indication, but chart indications must be used in connection with other signals and are not necessarily conclusive by themselves.

Rail and Industrial Averages may be kept on the same sheet for comparative purposes since they must confirm each other to determine a trend. When the averages follow each other over a period of days and make new highs or new lows at the same time, the trend (or change in trend) is confirmed.

The reasoning behind the well-known Dow theory that the rails must confirm the industrials in any major move is as follows: manufactured goods must be transported. It is increased production in the heavy industries (steel, machinery, etc.) which marks a sound, fundamental industrial improvement. This heavy freight is largely moved by rail rather than by truck or water. So the Railroad Average must reflect any sound upturn.

When the Rail and Industrial Averages are irregular in a trading range, they are preparing for a move. Analyze the volume to determine

*For an explanation of the technical terms used below, see the section on "Chart Formations" beginning on page 102.

whether it is accumulation or distribution. (Accumulation is on light volume, distribution on heavy volume.) The direction in which the averages start after leaving the trading area usually indicates the trend.

No absolute rule for averages can be set, but usually a definite resistance level is established halfway between the high and low of the move. For example, if the high of the move is 780 and the low 760, a resistance level would be met at about 770. Watch the market at this level. When volume diminishes or increases, but fails to break through, it shows important resistance. Most rallies only progress a third of the distance lost in the break before there is some kind of reversal. Should they penetrate the halfway point on volume, it indicates a continuance of the trend. If they make a double top and then fall off again, it indicates lower prices.

This same principle holds true in dips. Reactions usually retrace one-third to one-half of the distance attained by the rally. Anything more would indicate a continued downtrend. Support should be met at least at the halfway point, if not before. Double bottoms indicate that the market has reached bottom and will go no further. Watch the averages closely at this point. The reverse holds true of double tops. When the market makes a double top, it is likely to turn down from that point. Penetration of double bottoms shows excessive weakness and a continuation of the downtrend. Penetration of double tops shows great strength and a further upturn.

Always watch for a secondary reaction. When stocks plunge through a support or resistance level after stubborn persistence, they usually go further than if they merely slip through, especially when the move occurs on volume.

When the averages come back the full third or half of the rally within two or three days, it indicates short-covering rather than good buying, as the movement is too fast to be sound. It may be followed by another reaction. On the other hand, when there is covering from large or long-time shorts, there may be something in the wind. Any very vigorous short-covering should be carefully analyzed.

The Dow interpretation of the movement of market averages construes as fundamentally bearish the violation of previous lows by both the Industrial and the Railroad Averages. This is known as "a confirmation of the averages." The movement supposedly continues downward until both averages advance through previous recovery points, which would indicate a change of trend. The same principle holds true in reverse.

How to Keep and Use Charts

While the keeping of charts may be an exact statistical operation, reading them is largely a matter of individual reaction and personal interpretaiton, in which the psychological attitude of the chart-reader may play an important part. For this reason, even expert chart-readers often disagree. Chart-reading should not be considered infallible, but it is distinctly valuable as an aid in market analysis.

Charts should be used in connection with other market indicators. Charts are of the greatest assistance in determining resistance and support levels, in showing double and triple tops and bottoms, in estimating the probable extent of a rally or reaction, and in giving a picture of past action. On the other hand, they are undependable in a forced market or one which is under constant manipulation.

Which Charts to Keep

The ordinary trader should keep a daily chart of each of the stocks in which he is actively operating. Since the average operator should not work in over ten individual stocks, this should not impose too much of an obligation. All charts should date back not less than six months— a year is preferable. Subscription to a professional chart service may be secured if further detail is required.

Where the operator trades in a group of stocks of a particular industry, he should have a group chart for that industry. For example, if he is playing the steel stocks, he should chart five or six of the representative steels in a group chart. The same holds true of the utilities or any other group. It is then possible to assess the action of that particular industry by comparing its chart with the master charts of the Rail and Industrial Averages.

When the operator is carrying a group of stocks which are affected by any individual commodity, this should also be charted. For example, the price movement of wheat affects the agricultural-equipment and mail-order stocks and the movement of cotton affects textile stocks.

Method of Keeping Charts

Line and bar charts are made by drawing a vertical line for the movement of the stock each day, the top representing the high, the bottom the low, and a small cross-line which indicates the closing price.

No space should be left for Saturdays, Sundays, or holidays, as that would throw the trend lines out of adjustment.

The daily entries can be made in India ink. For contrast, trend lines may be drawn with red and blue pencil. These should also be used in outlining formations.

It is desirable that very important events be noted under the proper date at the top of the chart, to explain a sharp movement. Also, remember that volume is highly significant. It should always be entered at the bottom of the chart.

All charts should be dated each day. Charts on individual stocks should carry dividend dates.

Using the Charts

Never trade in a stock until you have watched its action on a chart. Note the highs and lows for the year, resistance points, support points. Does it act well in a falling market? Does it get support on drops? Does your chart show it to be under accumulation or distribution by group interests? This information is necessary before you trade.

When trying to evaluate any definite market move, consult the master charts showing the trend of the bond market and the Industrial and Rail Averages (see above).

Charts move on both fundamental and technical news. The long trend is based on fundamental conditions, minor movements on immediate news. News of a serious financial disturbance or some industrial condition of importance in either this or a foreign country would affect the major trend, at least for a time, inasmuch as it would have a direct effect on international conditions and our own commerce. The passing of some congressional measure, banking news, the action of a directorate in some important key industry, or an election of importance might affect the minor trend. It is also affected by technical conditions within the market itself, such as an oversold or an overbought condition, a large or small short interest, the wide fluctuations of some popular stock, professional trading of an unusual character, and other matters of this sort.

In every long-time trend there are important minor moves where trading profits can be taken, if good judgment is used. Whenever stocks have a sharp move in either direction, it will be followed by a reversal due to profit-taking. This offers an opportunity for trading if the operator is rapid in his movements.

During the period of accumulation at the end of a bear market, excellent opportunities are offered to the trader. The list swings back and forth within a given range and several points may be taken on small turns. This process is known as "backing and filling." By charting the outline of the trading area, the average limits of tops and bottoms are made clear.

Chart Formations

Correct reading of intricately detailed charts is a difficult and complicated study, but almost anyone can familiarize himself with the important formations and secure very material help. Chart formations may be divided into "basic" formations, which signal the end of a movement, and "intermediate" formations, which occur within a movement. The various formations are listed in Table 4. They may be described as follows:

Basic Formations

Head-and-shoulders formation. One of the most common of the chart formations is the "head-and-shoulders," so called because it has a long point in the center and lower points, or shoulders, on each side. In a perfect head-and-shoulders, the two shoulders are about equal and the spacing is practically the same on each side.

The left shoulder may form rather slowly, the head is usually made rapidly, in a sharp move, on volume, and the right shoulder should be completed in about half the time it took to form the left shoulder. In the formation of the right shoulder, when the depth of the "crotch" exceeds that of the base of the left shoulder, it indicates extreme violence in the move.

In a head-and-shoulders formation where the formation, supposed to be the head, breaks the trend line (see explanation), it confirms the opinion that this was the head of the formation.

TABLE 4

Chart Formations

BASIC CHART FORMATIONS

> *Indicating Accumulation:*
>> Head-and-Shoulders Bottom
>> Complex Bottom
>> Five-Point Formation (or
>>> Broadening Bottom)
>> Double or Triple Bottom
>> Ascending Bottom
>> Triangular Bottom
>> Common Upward Turn (or
>>> Rounding Bottom)

> *Indicating Distribution:*
>> Head-and-Shoulders Top
>> Complex Top
>> Five-Point Formation (or
>>> Broadening Top)
>> Double or Triple Top
>> Descending Top
>> Triangular Top
>> Common Downward Turn (or
>>> Rounding Top)

INTERMEDIATE CHART FORMATIONS

> Triangles
> Right-Angled Triangle, Ascending
> Right-Angled Triangle, Descending
> Isosceles or Symmetrical Triangle
> Spiral or Coil

> Gaps
> Common or Trading Gap
> Breakaway Gap
> Exhaustion Gap

After the second shoulder has been formed, the move continues in the direction taken by the last shoulder.

A head-and-shoulders *top* indicates distribution. A head-and-shoulders *bottom* indicates accumulation.

Complex formation. This is another and even stronger signal of the same type as the head-and-shoulders. It is practically a double head-and-shoulders, for it often has four or five points instead of three. The strength of this formation lies in the fact that it turns back repeatedly from a given point (top or bottom), showing repeated resistance. After making one extreme point, it fails to penetrate the preceding one, showing increasing resistance as the move continues.

A complex *top* indicates distribution. A complex *bottom* indicates accumulation.

Five-point formation (also called broadening top or bottom). This is a peculiar formation and occurs rarely. When it does appear, it is an almost indisputable signal. It consists of five distinct reversals in the move, each of which goes a little further than the preceding one. *The final move is a continuation of the fifth reversal.* It is practically unknown for it to reverse the sixth time.

The completion of the last turn in a five-point formation is a hard point to break, as it is a very strong resistance level. This last move is usually very rapid and is not subject to even minor setbacks. At times it starts off with a breakaway gap (see below).

After the last move of a five-point formation is completed and the directional move is under way, there is little opportunity for entering the market. It is therefore advisable to watch for this move very closely.

Double or triple top or bottom. This occurs where stocks drive again and again at a given top or base without breaking through. It is a strong signal for a reversal of the trend.

Ascending bottom. In this case, the chart formation takes on something of an upward curve, with the points at the bottom gradually ascending—that is, refusing to meet the previous lows. This formation frequently makes one side of a right-angled triangle. The direction of the sloping side being up, an upward movement is indicated.

Descending top. This is the exact opposite of the ascending bottom, for here the chart turns downward and each succeeding high is lower than the previous one. This, too, may develop into a right-angled triangle, and the sloping side, which points downward, indicates the direction of the movement.

Triangular top or bottom. This resembles the head-and-shoulders formation except that it does not have the wide swings which make the shoulders and the head. It is a culmination of a major move in the form of a triangle with a sharp apex. The triangular top indicates distribution; the triangular bottom, an upward move.

Common turn (also called rounding top or bottom). This is one of the most common formations. It is simply a gradual turning movement which forms a curve pointing in the direction of the coming movement. It is important in accordance with its size, including both width and depth. The turn occurs frequently in minor movements. Where it forms a rounding top, it indicates a lower market, a rounding bottom indicates higher prices.

Remember that the longer it takes to develop a formation, the stronger the formation and the more important the move before reversal.

Intermediate Signals

Triangles. Triangles are intermediate signals which appear in the movement somewhere between the start and the reverse. They represent a temporary halting-place where strength is being gathered for some more definite move. They may show either accumulation or distribution and are evidence of group action.

The *ascending right-angled triangle* signals a higher market. In this case, stocks are making higher bottoms each day and are refusing to drop to their old lows. The move shows distinct support and good buying. It presents a trend line pointing up.

The *descending right-angled triangle* signals a lower market. Stocks have repeatedly backed away from a given top without penetrating it, going lower with each movement. It presents a trend line pointing down.

The *isosceles or symmetrical triangle* shows a temporary resting-place in a period of accumulation or distribution, as the case may be. Except under very unusual circumstances, prices follow the previous trend when they break out of formation. The symmetrical triangle represents a retardation movement within the trend, offering a stabilization period before resumption of the move.

Spiral or Coil. The spiral, also known as the corkscrew or coil because of its peculiar formation, is a long or slow period of accumulation or distribution. It shows constant if irregular narrowing down of the range of prices. Some spirals cover a term of months. The longer the spiral, the more important the move. It shows group action.

When the spiral begins to form it covers quite a wide range, then gradually narrows down to a point or apex, from which it springs out into the move. It is not always possible to determine the direction of the move from the nature of the spiral formation. The previous trend must be considered. Watch the formation closely as it approaches the apex. The move usually continues in the direction in which it leaves the apex of the coil.

Occasionally false moves are used to shake out small operators before the major move is under way, so that operating groups may accumulate more stock. In the main, however, the spiral is a good indication of a major move.

Gaps. There are three kinds of gaps: the common or trading gap, the breakaway gap, and the exhaustion gap. Where a gap is not covered within a few hours, it is almost always an indication of a major movement in the direction of the original spread of the gap. Gaps usually appear at market opening.

The common or trading gap is really a spread between one day's prices and those of the next day. It comes in times of great irregularity, such as special accumulation or distribution. The market must be in a basically static position for the common gap, but on the surface there may be considerable irregularity and milling around. The gap's appearance most often is the result of some sudden news or some technical condition of the market itself, such as its being overbought or oversold. The gap should be closed within twenty-four hours and is frequently closed the same day. It is neither unusual nor of major importance, except for trading purposes. It gives the trader a fairly definite promise that he may buy or sell with the knowledge that the stock will return to its original price before the market closes. Common gaps can occur in either a bull or a bear market.

The breakaway gap is of more importance than the common gap. It usually appears at the beginning of a sharp directional move. It indicates either great weakness or great strength, according to the trend.

It frequently appears after the market has been artificially held, churns around for a period, and then breaks loose. It is either bearish or bullish according to the directional move. It marks the start of an important move and may not be covered for a long period. In most cases, however, it is closed by some sort of technical rally or reaction due to too fast a movement, after which the trend indicated by the gap is resumed.

To determine the importance of the breakaway gap, review the immediately preceding formations. If they include basic signals which confirm the gap, the breakaway indicates an important move. Breakaway gaps frequently follow a symmetrical triangle and often start a violent move.

The *exhaustion gap* is so called because it shows exhaustion after a long period of liquidation or rising prices. It signals the end of a long or violent directional move. Since a reversal of the trend usually follows it in a short time, it is covered quickly. It is a distinct warning to the operator to reverse his position.

Trend Lines

The trend line is a diagonal line which is established by connecting two or more important tops or bottoms. It should be drawn whenever possible, as it not only is a distinct guide to the direction of the market move but also serves as a diagonal line of resistance for stocks; under ordinary circumstances stocks are a sale when they touch the top of the trend line and a buy when they touch the bottom. (See below for a discussion of *horizontal* resistance lines which mark support and resistance levels.)

When a stock breaks through its trend line, use caution. It is a danger signal. A break-through on the downside indicates important selling. A break on the upside shows important buying and higher prices.

Special attention should be given to the trend in the Railroad Average. As a rule, this is a guide to all major trends. It is a virtual impossibility to have a major bull market in the industrials and a bear market in the rails.

When trend lines run at too sharp an angle, look for a reverse or at least a temporary change until prices are more fairly adjusted.

"Stop" a security where it breaks a trend line but do not short it until you see its action at that point.

√

Never buy a stock when it is near the top of its trend line.

Where a stock breaks down through a trend line and picks up volume, it is due for an important drop.

When the market breaks a trend line (either up or down) on volume, expect a continuation of that move.

Watch the top trend line in a bear market and the bottom trend line in a bull market.

Resistance and Support Lines

Resistance or support lines run straight across the sheet. They mark the points where stocks find resistance or support. They are very important in directional moves as they show where the move is likely to stop, or at least hesitate. Prices will fluctuate most of the time within the zone lying between the resistance line and the support line.

Reversals

The first indications of a change of trend occur when stock prices penetrate a resistance level after a major (or 50 per cent) correction. If market averages of individual stock prices reach this level in a reaction from a previous move (either up or down), watch closely; if they penetrate that level on volume, expect a continuation of the trend in that direction.

When stocks reverse any directional move (either up or down) and the reversal only covers one-third of the distance, the original trend is likely to resume. But when the reversal exceeds 50 per cent it indicates a change of trend, especially if the Rail and Industrial Averages confirm the move.

Closing prices usually indicate the trend for the following day.

Secondary Reactions

An important action is always followed by a secondary reaction which is often more pronounced than the first one. If the reaction exceeds half the distance of the recovery from the support levels, it shows weakness in the market structure. When it penetrates the lows of the previous movement, it definitely indicates that the immediate trend is down.

When buying or selling in a market move quiets down at a support or resistance level, watch carefully for big blocks. If they come out on the upside, it indicates buying; on the down side, selling. If there is no volume, it is difficult to determine the direction of the next move.

False Moves

False moves, lavishly used by group operators, may upset the calculations of the most skilled chartist, but they may often be detected through the following analysis:

If there is a move contrary to chart indications—for example, if the averages break on the upside out of a descending right-angled triangle—analyze the reasons for the upward move. If it is occasioned by some fundamental cause, your chart indications may be wrongly read or the market is changing its trend. If it is occasioned by some news of a temporary nature, or has no evident origin, consider it a false move against a fundamental trend.

Actually, the breaking of a critical point is invariably followed by a temporary move in the opposite direction. Later it is followed by the real move which was indicated by the breaking of the resistance point.

Part Four

TRADING WITH TICKER TECHNIQUE

12

MAKING THE TAPE WORK FOR YOU

In Part II the general rules for tape-reading were spelled out. In Part III the three main approaches to tape-reading were developed in detail. In this section, these general rules and broad approaches will be brought down to the specifics of trading. Before you start to trade, the basic ground rules discussed below must be grasped. Special emphasis is given to short selling, a somewhat neglected aspect of trading, but a necessary one if you are to trade actively at all times and in all markets.

Successful operators usually select certain stocks, limit their trading to those issues and concentrate on their action.

For quick trading, use an active stock with a small floating supply.

After you have taken a position in an intermediate move and determined your trend, decide on the probable swing of your stock and then do not follow the tape too closely. Determine about where you will buy or sell and let the market alone until that time approaches. Otherwise, hourly fluctuations will bias your opinion. *But always follow the general trend.*

Never let your losses run. If you are uncertain, "stop" your stock or get out. When a stock is not acting as you feel it should, sell and take your loss.

Never overstay the market. The public always does this. By the time the public enters the market, the cream of the profits has been taken. Professionals do not popularize a move until they are ready to get out.

Pay no attention to the openly expressed opinions of professional traders. They do not talk for publication when they are doing business.

113

When reports are spread on a stock or movement, it is usually propaganda. Few people advertise their movements except to their own advantage.

When you hear repeated news of the same character about any stock it is likely to be propaganda.

Stocks which rise rapidly fall rapidly.

Good buying is buying by important interests—banking, investment or institutional buying. Group accumulation is also valuable to an extent, as the group will hold for a profit.

Poor buying is short-covering or speculative buying for small profits.

Bottoms are more difficult to pick than tops. Stocks do not act alike on the tape and do not make their bottoms at the same time. Also, never forget that buying is a slower process than selling.

Remember that markets do not discount the same factor twice.

Sell on the *upward* scale. Professional traders distribute on the way up.

When you increase your holdings in a falling market to average your loss, you are bucking the trend. Never buck the trend; it is always unprofitable.

Trading by the Clock

If you plan to trade actively, it is important to have some understanding of the typical daily pattern of trading on the market. In some markets, for instance, buying in the afternoon may be wiser than putting your order in at the opening. Here are some guide-lines:

10:00 to 10:30	A strong opening usually slows down about 10:30. A weak opening frequently rallies after 10:30.
10:30 to 11:00	Often dull. If the opening has been strong, the market usually sells off a little. If weak at opening, it usually strengthens.
11:00 to 12:00	The market often has a little sell-off. Unless there has been a very weak opening this is frequently the best time of the day to buy. *But rally at this hour rarely holds.*

12:00 to 1:00   In a weak market, distress selling for overloaded margin accounts comes in at this hour. For that reason, in a bad market, any selling of importance at this time is likely to be distress selling.

1:00 to 2:00   The market is often inclined to irregularity. If it turns weak during this period, there will frequently be a strong close. When the market rallies, it often sells off again after 2:15.

2:00 to 2:15   If the market is on the upside, it is inclined to sell off just before 2:15. It comes back, sells off again from 2:35 to 2:45, and then turns upward. Profit-taking comes in between 2:35 and 2:45. If the market is in a downward trend, it usually runs up just before 2:15, falls off again, sells up from 2:35 to 2:45, then turns down. Short-covering comes in between 2:35 and 3:15.

2:15 to 2:30   When stocks hold firm through the afternoon to 2:15, they often react until about 2:30, when they turn upward. Traders take profits or cover short commitments around 2:30.

2:30 to 3:00   At 2:30 the market often reverses its action, except on very dull days. A rally after 2:00 o'clock is often followed by lower prices at 2:30; the market often closes on lows. A sell-off after 2:00 o'clock frequently means a sharp rally at the close.

Distress selling for overloaded margin accounts often comes in during the last hour.

"Day traders" never carry stocks overnight. They wait to see the action between 2:00 and 2:30, cover if they are short, and take their profits if they are long.

As a rule, the *highest* prices of the day are shown at the opening of the market, at noon, or at closing. The lowest prices of the day come most often at opening, between 11:00 and 12:00, or at close; 10:30 and 2:30 are also often times of low prices.

Between 12:00 and 1:00 any important selling can usually be traced to distress.

In a normal market, the best time to buy is between 11:00 and 12:00 or 2:00 and 3:00.

In a normal market, the best time to sell is at opening (where there has been a strong close the night before), between 1:00 and 1:30, and between 2:30 and 3:00.

In a trading market, where sudden news is likely to cause a swing, it is often advisable to close out all trades over the weekend.

In an uncertain market (particularly in a bear market), where certain stocks are singled out for targets in bear raids, they are often hit between 11:00 and 12:00.

A strong trend would be indicated by the following progression: a strong opening, reaction between 10:30 and 11:30, renewed strength from 12 to 12:30, a period of dullness, slight reaction from 1:30 to 2:15, a strong closing.

A weak trend would be shown by: a weak opening, a rally from 10:30 to 11:30, weakness from 12:00 to 1:00, strength until about 2:15, a weak closing.

Short Selling*

Some investors shy away from short selling. Admittedly, it is more hazardous than the usual long-side operation. Short selling often requires more frequent review, sometimes under pressure; but in some markets it can prove quite useful.

While it may be desirable to take a long-time short position at the beginning of what is likely to be a sustained bear market, it is usually inadvisable to do so. A short position is essentially a trading position.

Short sales should be made as nearly as possible at the peak of a sharp rally or the top of a bull market. When, after a long continued advance, stocks begin to rush up to new highs, slip back, start upward again; when volume increases at the top of the movement and prices churn without advancing; when trading becomes hectic and irregular, it is usually the end of the move and the market can be sold.

Conditions at the top of a long bull movement are perfect for short selling. The group operators have distributed most of their stock. The public bids eagerly. The professionals have "dressed up the market for the show" and, with prices sky-rocketing, things look rosy indeed. *This is the time to sell the market short.*

---

*For a thorough discussion of this subject, see THE TECHNIQUE OF SHORT SELLING—*Making Money on Declines in the Stock Market,* by Mark Weaver, published by Investors' Press, Inc., Palisades Park, N.J. 07650.

The public has bought the stocks at top prices from the professionals. When this hectic buying is over, stocks sag from lack of demand. Frightened purchasers see the market selling off and hurry to place more stop-loss orders, or sell "at market." The moment evident selling comes into the market, the public becomes panic-stricken. Stocks are thrown out in volume. Climax selling begins but there is no demand. Investment buyers are not interested for they know they will get the stocks much lower. The shorts have just completed their "short" portfolios. *There is no buying power.*

Yet some of the public remains optimistic. Also, the public is slower to accept a loss than the professional. Having bought stocks at the top, it hopes against hope that it may be possible to dispose of them on a rally. Instead of selling, it resorts to stop-loss orders. The technical position of the market is weak and there are no bids underneath it so the rally does not come. When the selling touches off the stops, the prices melt; the faster they melt, the heavier the selling. It is of such material that panics are made, and the only sure cushion under such a market comes when the shorts begin to cover.

Sell short when fundamental conditions do not warrant the advance or when you know that important bad news is just in the offing. *No market advances for any length of time against bad fundamental conditions unless it is at the turn at the bottom of a bear market.* When a market moves upward under such circumstances, it either means a distinct change of trend or else it is a forced market. *A forced market is a weak market,* and under ordinary conditions it can be sold.

Never sell short in a quiet market, where an apparent support level has been established, or against the major trend.

Quiet markets are dangerous. They are getting ready for a move. *The move may be up or down.* Stay on the sidelines until you know. After a downward move, when the volume of trading is low and prices stay just above support levels, an upturn is indicated.

Never sell short near the bottom of a bear market. This is especially true when there has been a long period of falling prices followed by irregularity and then a period of dullness. You will find the market very thin and stocks scarce. Irregularity means a change of trend, and dullness at the bottom of a market indicates accumulation. It is quite possible that stocks are being picked up by investors and placed in their strong-boxes. At such times, odd-lotters sell short heavily.

Actually, short selling is always heaviest when stocks approach the bottom, for the public grows frightened after a long period of liquidation and tries to recoup losses by selling short. When this happens, the market is about ready to turn.

On rare occasions, when the short position is large, certain stocks which are in demand are lent at a "premium." This means that the borrower must pay to the lender a certain specified amount each day for the loan of the stock. When the short position in the market is so large that a long list of stocks are being lent at premiums or become difficult to borrow, it is a signal that it is time to cover.

Short Covering

Never forget that when you are short you are in a vulnerable position, for you have sold something which you do not own. Economically this is unsound. Bear it in mind and move quickly.

Never stay short after the short interest becomes very large. Any good news is likely to cause a covering movement, and an important rally may develop into a short-squeeze when stocks are scarce.

Always cover a short position when major pivotal stocks make new lows. Professional shorts cover under those circumstances, and a technical rally follows. You can short again higher if you wish to replace your position.

Under any circumstances, cover your shorts before the market reaches absolute bottom. Stock then becomes scarce.

When the market reverses itself quickly after a sudden drop, *cover shorts at once* (except on a high market opening). Never let your losses run. If for some reason you have not been able to cover and stocks have been crowded up to a boiling-point against the shorts, wait until the major excitement is over and the market slips off again. Sharp short covering weakens the technical structure of the market. In punishing the shorts the bulls often punish themselves.

When an operating short seller finds himself in a bad position in a sharp rally, it is usually best (if there is no fundamental reason for the rally—and many rallies are psychological) to stay short until the rally begins to weaken. Few rallies last more than three days without a reaction, especially when they have no fundamental economic cause.

How to Spot Short Covering

In a market where there is a heavy short interest and where prices do not decline during the noon period, the shorts are often frightened and cover about 2:15 or near the close.

The man who is covering his "shorts" is naturally in greater haste than the man who is buying for a long account. Any favorable news makes the short seller hurry to cover, for he foresees a rally, whereas the investor is not rushed and bides his time to buy.

Fast comebacks after a reaction are almost always short covering and speculative buying.

In order to determine the difference between short covering and buying for the long account, watch the volume, the rapidity of the price changes, and whether activity is in the stocks which are popular with the shorts.

When it is good buying, the blocks are large and are taken at steadily increasing prices. When the market slows down and the blocks become smaller, there is no weakness. Only in rare cases do large blocks appear at lower prices. After the rally has continued for some time, there is likely to be a period of dullness. If prices then go higher and the volume continues on the upside, it indicates buying for a turn. A rally of this sort should continue for about three days.

When it is *short-covering*, stocks will move up rapidly. Popular trading stocks may jump from half to more than a point between sales. If it is an inconsequential rally, the volume is small, for the big shorts will not cover. The market then slows down after the first outburst, goes dull, becomes irregular, and begins to slip off. When the volume begins to increase on the downside, the rally is over.

Much of the short covering is done "at market." This is what makes a "boiling" market.

Watch the volume on these short covering rallies. If the blocks are large, the big shorts think it important enough to cover. This should be a signal to the small operators to do likewise.

Very little good buying comes into a short covering rally. Wise investors buy more thoughtfully, at definite prices.

When there is doubt as to whether it is a genuine rally or short covering, check the stock prices and the volume, especially the latter.

If the volume was out of proportion and the price changes were equally so in issues where there was a large short interest; *and if the rest of the list shows comparatively little change,* it was short covering and the market will slip down again. If, however, the volume and price changes were over a broad front and included "investment stocks," then in all probability there was good buying and the rally was significant.

13

SPOTTING LONG-TERM TRENDS
THROUGH FUNDAMENTALS

No tape-reader would advocate exclusive reliance on the readings of the tape. Again and again, the successful tape-readers of the past have indicated that you should learn all you can about the general direction of the market and the individual stocks in which you trade. This section presents a brief checklist of the important non-technical factors that might influence the market.

Fundamental Factors

Fundamental influences on the market may be classified under three general headings: business conditions, commodities, and money.

Business conditions. Major trends are both foreshadowed and stimulated by such factors as inventory levels, machine-tool orders, consumer sales, unemployment levels, and production rates in relation to seasonal norms.

Commodities. Close attention should be given to the state of the commodity market. Wheat and cotton are especially important. The price of wheat not only affects the entire market but is particularly reflected in agricultural-equipment and mail-order stocks. When wheat prices turn lower, stocks usually follow suit. The same holds true in a

121

lesser degree for cotton. A bull market rarely gets under way until commodity prices are on the upturn.

Money. Lower rediscount rates stimulate an upturn in the stock market, as does a lower rate for call money. A high rediscount rate and high call money often precede a drop in the market.

Commercial paper is another indicator. When a sharp decline in commercial paper rates brings them below the yield of average high-grade bonds, this is followed by a sharp rise in the averages of stock prices.

The action of bank stocks is an important trading signal. When bank stocks decline, the general market will follow. When they rise, stock prices will do better.

Signs of a Major Uptrend

1. *Business conditions:*
Inventories are low and producers are short of raw materials.
Machine-tool industries note a growing demand for their products.
Unemployment is on the wane and factory payrolls rise.
Orders for railroad equipment assume substantial proportions.
Freightcar loadings increase.
Power production and consumption rise.
Scrap steel prices go up.
Automobile production exceeds seasonal volume.
Department store sales show an increase above seasonal expectations.
Real estate is in demand.
Exports increase.

2. *Commodities:*
Commodity prices stabilize and then turn upward—especially wheat and cotton.
Steel ingot and finished-steel production increases.
Copper prices rise.
Chemicals are in good demand.
Coke, bituminous coal, rubber, zinc, and gas production rises.
Wool and pork are increasingly in demand.

3. *Money:*
Gilt-edged securities have been selling at yields considerably more than the cost of money. The ratio of brokers' loans to stock

prices is low and brokers' loans fall as common stock prices rise.
Money is cheap and credit good.
Buying on credit is down sharply.
Bond prices have turned upward.
Stock prices bear a reasonable ratio to earnings.
Flotations are not excessive.
The rediscount rate is low.

Signs of a Major Downtrend

1. *Business conditions:*
Business indicators have reached a crest and show signs of turn-
    ing downward.
Machinery orders diminish.
The demand for railroad equipment is on the wane.
Freight car loadings continue to decrease.
Power production and consumption slip steadily lower.
Scrap steel prices fall off.
Automobile production sinks below seasonal volume.
Department store sales show a continual drop.
There is a lower demand for real estate.

2. *Commodities:*
Commodity prices turn weak, especially wheat and cotton.
Steel output diminishes measurably.
The demand for copper decreases.
Orders for agricultural chemicals show a steady decrease.

3. *Money:*
Bank stocks continue to decline.
Bond sales lag and prices are low.
Commercial loans reach a crest and turn down.
Credit is strained and money rates are high.
Corporate financing is excessive.
Call money and time rates are high, and the rediscount rate shows
    a constant increase.

There is a bad adjustment between stock prices and investment
values; stock yields and current interest rates; stock prices and their
earnings.

14

HOW TO GET STARTED WITH
TICKER TECHNIQUE

There is one thing common to all of the methods of tape-reading outlined in this book: they all attempt to forecast the future level of prices on the basis of the most recent trading action of a stock. Anyone willing to base his buying and selling orders primarily on the pattern of actual stock transactions is clearly a "tape-reader" and should be able to profit from a thorough study of the techniques for spotting meaningful price and volume patterns in stock transactions.

One common mistake made by stock market operators just beginning to pay closer attention to the actual pattern of stock transactions is an attempt to cover too many stocks. Trying to cover the waterfront, these novice tape-readers follow many stocks superficially and none adequately. It is far better to know a few stocks well than to have a nodding acquaintance with a large number. Choose your methods carefully and give realistic consideration to the time you will have, week in and week out, to apply these methods. Often attempts to cover too much ground can result only in frustration—an impressive array of data for the early weeks, blanks for the current weeks, and no firm basis for current buying and selling decisions.

Trade only in those stocks that conform to definite rules and habits. Disregard those that do not move according to your method. There are dozens of possible market patterns. If among the stocks you attempt to follow a few always turn out to be "foolers," avoid these stocks. No method works equally well with all stocks. Keep active in those stocks that move in line with your methods.

Few market traders rely exclusively on tape action in making their decisions. Earnings, new products, balance sheets, management changes cannot help but influence your attitude toward a given stock. But if you wish to make the best use of ticker technique, any news about a stock should be judged chiefly by its effects on the market action. Using ticker technique, news in itself is not important and should never be the basis for buying or selling a stock. It is the reaction to the news that forms the basis for going into a situation or getting out.

This approach has several advantages. It brings a sense of needed objectivity into your market operations. One of the most difficult factors that every investor has to contend with on the market is his own emotions. Buying on news or a favorable balance sheet, without proper allowance for the action of a stock, leaves you open to surprises. After a minor move in response to the news, many stocks have an unhappy tendency to go dead. This leaves you with a dull stock after entertaining high hopes. Proper appraisal of the trend and pattern of the stock prior to the good news and during the period when it becomes public knowledge can often help you avoid time-wasters in your buying.

Perhaps the most useful clue that can come from ticker technique is insight into the following or sponsorship that a stock is capable of attracting. Few stocks can make much headway, regardless of how bright their futures appear, until they have developed an active market following. Stocks that trade only a few hundred shares a week and move narrowly within a range are unlikely to arouse much interest on the market in the early stages of any change in the fundamentals of their operations. These stocks may make good long-term investments, but they require patience.

On the other hand, stocks with active followings often move quite quickly in response to sudden reversals in their fortunes. And it may take fairly modest bits of good news to touch off worthwhile moves in their market prices. If you wish to follow active stocks, you have little choice but to acquire a working knowledge of their price and volume patterns.

If you have decided that the use of ticker technique can be helpful in deepening your knowledge of stocks and add an important dimension to your overall trading procedures, these are several simple rules that will help you get started:

(1) Select a method. Keep in mind your time limitations. It is obviously impossible for most of us to follow the live tape. This still leaves you with a fairly wide range of choices—from reporting services that provide printed records of every transaction to weekly stock tables. Another way to save time is to limit yourself to a few stocks, especially in the early stages of your learning process.

(2) Having selected a method for following the market action of stocks that fits your time requirements, study this method carefully. Re-read the appropriate pages in the earlier chapters of this book. Know what you are looking for. Boil your insights down to a few simple patterns and locate these patterns in the recorded action of stocks.

(3) Test your methods a while on paper. Find out if your patterns actually seem to work out as predicted. Consider expressing these patterns on charts. Charting will increase the time necessary to follow your stocks, but some stock market operators see patterns more clearly when they are plotted.

(4) Test your methods with an actual commitment of cash. During this trial run, consider odd-lots. The size of the commitment is often less important than the fact that you are using real money and making live decisions. This is often the acid test of a stock market method. With their money actually riding on a situation, many investors find that their emotions often play them false. It is one thing to trade on paper, it is another to make a cash purchase and suffer through the second-guessing that inevitably follows.

(5) If you have successfully come through these first four steps with flying colors, you may look on yourself as a full-fledged tape-reader and a graduate user of ticker technique. You should now be in a position to increase the size of your average commitment and hold your own in a wide variety of actual markets.

(6) But there is one final rule that could be most important of all —never be dogmatic. Never argue with the tape. If a situation turns against you, cut your losses short and try again. Remember, few traders buy at the absolute bottom and few sell at the absolute top, but there

are usually many profitable opportunities in between these extremes in an actively traded stock.

There are three factors commonly used in appraising the worth of a stock—its quality, its price, and its trend. Quality gives a clue to the defensive nature of a company and its stock. Generally speaking, quality alone cannot make money for you, but it may save you money in a rapidly deteriorating market. But quality stock can make money for you if the price is right and the trend is favorable.

Price is a dependent variable. No stock is cheap at any price unless it is moving in a clearly defined channel. You cannot make money, either short or long, in a stock that is dawdling. This clearly leaves the trend as the most important consideration for profitable stock market operations.

Ticker technique is the most developed method for arriving at an appraisal of the current trend of a stock. A trend once in place continues until reversed. Judicious use of ticker technique can spot a trend once it is established and sound the alarm bell when the trend falters. Few seasoned traders would venture far without knowing the current trend of their situation, and neither should you. Know your stocks; know how they act; and you will be in a position to plan your portfolio for profits rather than hold it on the chance that it may work out over time. If you like active stocks, the time spent learning the ABC's of ticker technique can pay handsome dividends.